26 WAYS TO BREAK A

WEIGHT LOSS PLATEAU

26 WAYS TO BREAK A

WEIGHT LOSS PLATEAU

Stop the Dieting Frustration and Get Fascinated with Your Fitness Habits

ANDREW BIERNAT

Your Personal Growth Personal Brand Podcast. Designed for ambitious, growth minded professionals, this podcast helps Grow Getters like you take their game to the next level. You'll get to learn from the experts as host Andrew Biernat asks the questions you've always wanted to know. We'll cover topics from health, to mindset, to productivity, and business.

DEDICATION

I dedicate this book to all of those I know that are struggling to lose weight. The challenge can seem insurmountable at times and I hope this book can provide some guidance and relief as you pursue one of the greatest personal transformations of your life.

AUTHOR'S NOTE

This book was the catalyst for my own personal change. I wrote this book in early 2021 during a time of restrictions in the fitness industry. Exhausted from the ups and downs of lockdowns, outbreaks, and intense cleaning and distancing procedures, I was burnt out. This book was my last-ditch attempt to stay engaged and energized in a time of uncertainty.

As I finished this book and launched a matching Masterclass I became aware of one important thing: I needed to take my message of personal growth beyond the fitness industry. So I did.

I changed careers, started a business, and launched a podcast. All while celebrating the new addition of our second child, Sophia.

In this new edition I've removed the Masterclass and kept the focus on just what appears in the book. While you'll see me refer to clients in the present tense throughout this book, know that I no longer work directly in the fitness industry with these individuals.

I hope this book can be a catalyst for change for you as it has been for me.

CONTENTS

PART II

FOCUSED BREAKTHROUGH

CONTINUOUS IMPROVEMENT

INTRODUCTION

I hate seeing people get stuck on their weight loss journey, especially when they give up and stay stuck. This book will get you moving in the right direction to give you the momentum and results you need to keep going. I've had many times in my life where I haven't had momentum. It felt like swimming through quicksand. Each attempt I made to fix things felt like a step backward in progress.

I lived in Buffalo, New York for a few years. It was a wild time of my life and I got lost in my own selfish pursuits. I had been teased in high school for being too skinny. After college my love of McDonald's and beer guzzling had pushed me far from the trim six pack I was used to.

After losing my job due to my lack of focus I had an opportunity for self-reflection. What I saw staring back surprised me.

I was closing in on sixty pounds heavier than I had been in high school and it wouldn't be long before the bulge at my waist turned into a full-fledged beer belly. I had put on enough weight that my older brother, who was significantly more muscular, started calling me his big brother. Jobless, lonely, and lost I knew I needed a change.

It took me moving out of Buffalo and changing careers in order for me to break out of that rut. I was stuck both physically and mentally.

My change of careers brought me into the fitness industry. I had to embody the things I was learning before I could feel comfortable teaching them. The road was rough but was accelerated compared to what many suffer through. I want to show you a faster way to get and stay in shape.

The goal for you is to break out of your rut and finally start losing weight again. There's a million and one ways to do that. I'll give you the easiest and simplest right here, right at the beginning. Are you ready? It's going to blow you away.

Just stop eating for three days in a row. And your weight loss plateau will be over.

Boom, problem solved.

Now I think you're recognizing that that's probably not a good idea.

It's not even an average idea.

It's a pretty terrible idea because that is temporary.

What I want to teach you is how to never plateau again or at the very least if you do, you'll know the steps to follow to get back on track. I want to give you a word of caution. If you skim through or don't finish this book, what you'll get is an idea or two, and you may test them and you may find that they work very, very well for you, but you will be missing out on the bigger picture. And the next time you get stuck, those one or two ideas that you learned may not serve you.

What will you do then?

Right now, you're probably struggling with a lack of motivation. You may not know where to start. Maybe you're feeling apathetic, or maybe you're convinced that nothing will work. Maybe you're already doing everything perfect. And you just can't imagine why things aren't working.

Perhaps you've got a lot of pent up emotion.

Maybe you're feeling sad, depressed, angry, frustrated, disappointed, skeptical, or scared.

Or maybe you're excited and ready to embrace new ideas and opportunities.

There are two paths ahead of you right now.

One is the path that you're already on. You can keep going. And you've probably got a good idea where that leads.

The other path?

Flows through the rest of this book into your bright, beautiful future.

The following pages of this book are for those who are committed to losing weight.

Whether you are feeling committed right this moment or not, you will be committed by the end of this book.

If I could sum up the biggest takeaway that I want to bestow upon you, it is this: that you need to keep working at it.

Even if results aren't showing up right away, persevering through the difficulty and finding ways to adapt these strategies that I'm about to give you is what's going to ultimately get you your results. This is not a cookie cutter program. This is not a follow step A and then step B and then step C for your magical weight loss results.

What you need to do is learn, absorb, test, and continue to grow and experiment. I'm going to show you at least 26 ways to do that. And I'm going to give you the encouragement that you need, especially in those dark times, those hard times, those times when things just aren't going your way. You'll be able to continue and power through and see results you thought only other people could get.

I was put on this earth to help people achieve breakthroughs and to bring joy to those that I interact with. Hopefully we get to grow together on this journey. And my hope, my sincerest hope, is that you achieve the breakthroughs that you're looking for. You're going to learn the secret strategies to keep your momentum going. You'll also learn the tactics, the small stuff that's going to help you lose weight and keep it off for good.

PART I

CHAPTER ONE

The Reason Your Weight Loss is Like Drilling for Oil

Let's start with the basics. You want to experience more weight loss. You see before you an endless possibility of choices. You may feel paralyzed, overwhelmed, or worse yet you may find yourself misled and convinced into any number of weight loss schemes where you are not the primary benefactor.

There is no one way to get the results you want, but there is a surefire way to not get the results you want.

Want to know what it is?

It's to go on a diet.

Dieting is synonymous with failure. A diet is temporary, like a new shirt. When it goes out of fashion, you'll be left with the same body you had before.

Many diets are well meaning. They seek to supply a nutritional framework for people to follow.

Unfortunately, what happens is that people follow the program as long as it's convenient. At some point a person will stop following the plan and slowly slide back into old habits. Losing ground and regaining weight along the way.

I've seen this happen too many times to count and it makes me want to pull my hair out.

The end result of dieting is frustration.

Dieting results in stagnation and they are never long-term solutions meaning that most diets end without true success.

I know what you're thinking. You've had successful diets before. You lost tons of weight and it changed your life.

And yet here you are, reading a book about weight loss.

That diet at best got you to a new plateau. At worst it left you high and dry and wishing for results that never seemed to materialize.

I've noticed a pattern. I'll see someone finally get fed up enough with their condition to do something about it. They find the first thing that pops up and it's usually some sort of diet. They hop on the diet; they find some success. They're excited. They begin to lose weight. At some point, things go awry and they either stop dieting or they hit a plateau. As the diet fades their old habits start coming back. And any progress that they made slowly starts creeping back onto their bodies.

I noticed that some clients were different, and I wondered why. What makes these clients successful and how do they continue to see success even years after they had lost their weight?

How do they maintain it? How do they get there?

And how can I help other people to do the same?

What's special about these clients is not that they found the perfect diet. It's not that they found the perfect plan. It's not that they had the best trainer.

Something different is going on in their minds. Weight loss and maintenance just becomes the way they live their life. It took a while for me to put my finger on what the one thing was that sets these people apart.

Are you ready to learn what it is?

Do you want to know that one thing?

The one thing is continual adaptation.

It is the commitment to learning and growing and shifting and changing as conditions around you continue to change.

In the second half of this book, there are 26 different ideas, different thoughts, and processes that you can follow and experiment with. What we've found is these processes work. When people commit to them and practice them, they work.

However, not all of them will work for you. And not all of them will work right away. What you need to do is decipher which strategy you need at which time.

That is the purpose of the first half of this book. You'll be getting your head on straight and figuring out what you need to be targeting first.

I want you to look back on some of your most successful times in weight loss,

This was when everything was going your way. The weight seemed to be melting off. It was almost easy. You felt like you were unstoppable. If you've never felt these feelings, imagine what they would feel like.

What was different about that time versus now? And then what happened that caused you to stop losing weight? What caused that transition?

For many people it happened because they were doing the same thing and they expected different results. If you're drilling for oil and you hit a gusher, tap into that and ride it all the way to the bank. Just like with weight loss, if you find a sustainable long-term strategy that you love and is getting you results, keep going with it!

If the oil stops coming up, what are you going to do? Are you going to drill in the same spot? Or are you going to find a new spot to drill for oil? Many people believe that finding a new diet or finding a new plan is like finding a new oil field, but what you're really doing is you're drilling a hole right next to the last one. And what you're going to find is what you found last time, except you won't see the results as quickly as you did that first time. You're not going to find success like you found that first time. It will slip through your fingers like dry sand pumped from an empty well.

I'm going to share a story about one of my most successful clients. Her name is Cindy. Cindy has been working with me for well over five years. We've gotten to know each other very well. We've seen each other through many ups and downs. And Cindy's case, though unique to her, is not a unique situation.

She was overweight. She was fed up. She was tired and she was ready for a change. She worked her tail off at her job. She cared deeply about her husband. But she wanted to see change in her life.

But turn after turn, and attempt after attempt, she found that things just weren't working. She came to work with us and I could tell within the first few months of working with her, that she was going to do great things.

I couldn't place my finger on what was different at the time, but I can now, what was different about Cindy was she just kept trying. She kept testing. She showed up to every seminar and I saw her absorbing every lesson we taught in class.

There were many times where Cindy found herself at a plateau where things stopped working for a bit, but she didn't give up. Cindy kept trying, kept testing, and kept experimenting. And what she found was continued weight loss.

The weight loss wasn't constant, nor was it easy, but the weight came off. Cindy has been maintaining her best weight for years now. She's had a couple of fluctuations due to work stress, but those were ironed out because she finds a way to adapt. She continues to overcome.

Cindy is not a special case. Cindy could be you. My hope is that through the rest of this book, you will absorb the strategies, the mindset, and the will to see yourself through to the end. I want you to get to maintenance, to celebrate the change that you have created within yourself.

When I was younger, one of my favorite cartoons was Inspector Gadget. Inspector Gadget, or Gadget for short, was a goofy, ridiculous man who had way too many tools at his disposal. Gadget seemed to have a different device for every single scenario, like the cartoon version of MacGyver.

Every time Gadget got stuck, he found a way out. He was accompanied by his niece, Penny, who was the common sense of the operation and tended to be the one who ultimately solved the problem and beat the bad guys.

You are like Penny. You are going to be the common sense that gets the job done. I'm your Inspector Gadget. I'll be providing the toolkit for you to turn to when you get into a jam.

Right now, it may feel like the only tool you have is a hammer. You keep searching for a nail to hit but things just aren't working. You need some different tools. You need a new way of doing things.

That is what will help you reignite your weight loss and break through your plateau.

CHAPTER TWO

Seeing Your Old Weight Loss Tactics for What They Really Are... Old

You are going to discover that this book is different from any other plan you've been given. That's why you're here. You're tired of the same cycle and you're ready to break out of what ultimately hasn't been working for you. What has gotten you to where you are today has not gotten you to where you want to go, at least not for long.

You want to go further. You want to see more change and you are ready to make that investment in yourself to make it happen. You may have been down this road before where someone promises you the moon and the stars, and they deliver a pile of dirt. My hope is that you are able to take these principles and procedures and incorporate them into your daily life. You will turn this knowledge, these tactics, and these broader strategies into a way of life and a lifestyle that lasts a lifetime.

You may recognize your pattern. You may know that you get excited. You get thrilled when you have a new plan. And eventually that plan starts to work and you see progress happening. But at a certain point, the progress stops. The momentum fades, and the world turns gray.

It's at that point, that things start to slip away. You lose your enthusiasm, you lose your momentum and your energy, and you start falling back into old habits that eventually bring you to where you are right now. You may have been through that cycle many times, and there is an industry that makes a tremendous amount of money because you do.

That's the way the diet industry thrives, not by actually fully solving people's problems, but by offering new solutions to the problem they keep having over and over again. My hope is that you never have this problem ever again.

There are many things that people start to pursue when they're working on losing weight. Dieting is one of many.

You may be the type to try doing the same thing you did when you were 20.

Perhaps you'll just work harder.

Or maybe you're looking to see what your friends and coworkers are doing.

I know that with this plan you're going to be able to push past all the old baggage that you're carrying. And you'll be able to start fresh and move in a new direction. Those old strategies didn't work, even if it seemed like they did, because ultimately those old strategies have brought you to where you are today. And today you are still seeking a change.

One of my clients, we'll call her Gloria, was on the cheerleading team in high school. And she has carried that energy and enthusiasm throughout the rest of her life. She has a spring in her step and a smile on her face. When Gloria gets stuck, she tends to fall back into her old ways of doing things. Her old way of doing things: Just do more, just work harder, eat a little bit less, run a little bit more.

At one point, it was an extremely effective strategy, which is why she revisits it in times of need. Gloria is no longer 20. What worked when she was 20, seems to be working less and less as the years go by. Her knees are hurting more. And she's discovering that the quick diet tricks don't work like they used to.

Eventually, all tactics will become obsolete and ineffective.

In the chapters ahead you'll learn what it takes to lose your excess weight and maintain that for the long term.

CHAPTER THREE

The Real Reason
Your Diets Always Fail
(Hint: It's More Profitable That Way)

You've been continually lied to by professionals. I know that's a bold claim but hear me out. I hate to say it about people in my same field, but many fitness and health professionals are unaware of the broader implications of what they're teaching. I don't need you to pay me to make your meals for you. I don't want you to take a course from me out of desperation. My hope is that you learn from me because you see the need in your life, and you see that you're ready for change.

People spend hundreds and even thousands of dollars every year chasing after weight loss pipe dreams sold by snake oil salespeople. And many of these people are nice people caught up in a system designed for one thing: profit.

What's the best kind of customer?

A repeat customer.

What's the best way to keep someone coming back?

Get them hooked in a cycle of dependence where your solution is the only answer.

From cigarettes, to alcohol, to the original Coca-Cola, dependence is a great revenue stream. These types of companies used chemical dependence as their method of profit. What the diet industry has done is so much more nefarious.

They have created a system that virtually guarantees they will stay in business forever.

Most diets fail within a year. The research I've seen has ranges from 60% all the way up to 95% failure rates. The failure rate was higher the longer the studies lasted.

If casinos played with those kinds of odds they'd be outlawed.

Diets are designed to get you short term success. You get to become a shining testimonial. For three months. And then reality hits and you gain back any weight you may have lost.

The tricky thing about the weight loss industry is that they only need to create the illusion of successful and happy customers. They need some people to have initial success and then they sell it like crazy. Meanwhile, like a Ponzi scheme waiting to pop, the first customers start to realize they've been hoodwinked. By the time enough people get wise to the diet's shortcomings, there's a new fad sweeping the nation that promises to fix everything that the last diet failed at.

Think back over your lifetime the number and type of diets you've seen. Macrobiotic, Atkins, Mediterranean, Paleo, Keto, Beverly Hills, Slim Fast, Dexatrim, Liquid, Zone, South Beach, Intermittent Fasting, and countless others have come and gone.

How come nobody is jumping on the Beverly Hills diet anymore? Why don't people do the liquid diet like Oprah recommended in the 1980's?

The answer my friend, is that they don't work.

Diets come and go because people try one, fail, and then look for something else that scratches that same itch. Many of my clients can no longer even count the number of diets they have tried.

Diets are designed to be temporary. They are designed to get you whipped into a buying frenzy where you get the cookbook, sign up for meal plan, and buy every book on the subject.

If you actually had success that lasted, it would be a great tragedy for the industry. You would no longer be a repeat customer. But you know what? They don't care. Because they know that almost no results from diets are permanent. They can call you a success story, and then just bide their time as they wait for you to slide back to where you were before.

They'll embrace you with open arms as they pick your wallet and sell you the newest trend.

The diet industry thrives on the failure of its customers.

That's not the way I roll. I seek long lasting results for my clients and one of the hardest things I do is help people break out of the diet mentality.

Want to know the mentality that you need to have in order to find success?

Let me tell you about a client of mine named Tom. I was working as an assistant trainer at the time and he was one of the first people

I got to see go through a weight loss journey from start to 'finish'. I put finish in quotes because maintenance never ends.

Tom was a hard worker at the school where he worked, but he was coming up on retirement years. As Tom prepared for his golden years, his wife was worried about his long-term health. Tom was obese and his wife wanted many more decades with him.

She brought him to a seminar we were hosting, against his will, so I'm told. At the end of the seminar, we had people visualize where they were headed in the future if they took the advice we were giving them. And then we had them envision what their life would look like if they didn't make any changes.

This activity convinced Tom that he needed to do something, so he begrudgingly agreed to work with us for a month.

His initial plan was to placate his wife, maybe lose a few pounds, and then do things his own way. He ended up losing almost 100 pounds in total. He worked with us for almost a year, with his plan being to get the jumpstart he needed and then take off and fly on his own.

His initial start with us was very promising. His first month he lost eight pounds, a great sustainable number to push for. His second month he lost zero. Tom felt the wind go out of his sails. He felt like he was dead in the water. He didn't know what to do.

He knew that he needed something different. Tom kept pushing. Tom kept trying. He learned new tricks. He tested new principles and the following month he was losing again. Tom did not lose his weight in a nice, easy, straight line down. Tom went through what I would call a typical weight loss journey.

Some months were incredible, some months were okay, and some months were disappointing. He even had a couple months where he gained slightly, but by the end of a year, Tom was a different man. After eighteen months Tom had lost over 75 pounds.

Tom had control of his life and he started envisioning the future past retirement and that's when things started to get really exciting.

Since Tom retired as band director from the local high school, he has gone on to become a professor at a renowned local university and has created musical scores for films and video games. He teaches his students to do the same.

Tom still works out five days a week and he continues to learn and adjust his habits so that he can sustain and maintain his progress.

You might just need some initial momentum. You might need that quick start. And maybe that check-in once in a while. That's what Tom needed. We have many clients that call themselves 'lifers' because they won't leave our programs because they love the results they've gotten, and they feel like they are still able to continue and improve.

Whatever path lies ahead for you, I know that this book can be a game changer for you.

CHAPTER FOUR

The Side Effect of Weight Loss That Will Make You a Better Spouse and Friend

Something amazing happened for me when I decided to make a change in my life. Unfortunately, some bad things have happened to me because I was unwilling to change.

My first unwanted change was losing my job.

The second was the opportunity that presented itself next.

In my job searching I was seriously considering moving South. I've lived in upstate New York my whole life and the winters are a little grating. A question came up the other day that made me realize how differently we think around here. Someone said it was supposed to snow and it was supposed to snow between one and three.

People immediately responded between one and three inches or one and three feet?

The answer was one to three inches.

At which point everyone lost interest and went about their day.

Snow here is a normal part of life, just like setbacks and hardship is a normal part of life. And I wanted less of both!

When I made the change in career, it was because of an offer from my brother. He offered to bring me on as a personal training assistant so that I could learn, help him and grow his business.

At the same time, I was interviewing for a sales job and the pay differential between the two jobs was substantial. I stopped by my brother's studio early one morning to follow along and see what it was like. Compared to my stuffy corporate job that I had before, this place felt like an energy and enthusiasm wonderland. I was shocked at how kind and hardworking everyone was.

Later that day I had my last interview for the sales job.

By the time I was done with the interview, I knew where I had to be.

I was reluctant to become a trainer. Clearly, I didn't look like a trainer. I had no initial passion for the subject, outside of my failed attempts to make myself look better. And I was starting off at the very bottom. Taking a job where the starting pay was minimum wage was a tough pill to swallow as a college grad with debt that seemed ready to swallow me whole.

Change can be a tricky thing.

Change can come and take us, kicking and screaming.

Or we can be the agents of change in our own lives. Like an ever-changing city skyline, sometimes destroying something good to make way for something better.

My biggest obstacle was the fifty pounds I had found since high school. I weighed in at about 210 pounds, and I normally weighed under 160.

I needed to lose some weight. I also needed to become a person of authority and someone that other people could look up to. I don't know about you, but I tend to smile nicely and move on when a professional, who clearly doesn't practice what they preach, tells me what to do.

In the ensuing year I learned, I tried, I adapted, I shifted, and I changed. My physical condition changed faster in that year than I thought possible.

It was because I brought my focus onto my health. I made a commitment to making the changes and I knew, I just knew, deep down that no matter what I was going to get results. I had spent so much of my time hiding who I was. I had spent a significant amount of time trying to be someone else.

As I lost weight and as my fitness and physique improved, I found my mood changed a bit as well. I became more comfortable with myself. I became more okay with being who I was.

At some point in that physical change I began to love the way I looked and felt. Another strange thing started happening.

I started working on my mind and my emotions.

That work was twice as hard as working on my body. The rewards of which are still paying dividends to this day.

Through the help of a professional plus countless books, seminars, and all kinds of other ways of absorbing material, I shifted the way I saw the world. I shifted the way that I took care of myself and I became the type of person that did a better job of taking care of others. My struggle with authenticity brought me to a crossroads. I decided that I was healthy enough physically and mentally to start dating again.

I can remember the first few dates with my now wife and how I was thinking of how I could share more of my life with her. And I knew that authenticity needed to be the basis for our relationship, for our connection.

My old way of living was to be who the other person needed me to be. But I knew that was not going to work for either of us for the long term. If she was going to love me and connect with me it was going to be because of who I really was.

By the end of our first month together, I decided I was going to tell my future wife my whole backstory.

all the darkness, all the bad stuff, as well as some of the good stuff.

In doing so I anticipated that she would become my future ex-girlfriend.

I wanted to give her the chance to accept me as I was because I had seen the tremendous change that I had gotten by accepting myself as I was. I knew that if I was going to have a successful future relationship with this woman, that she needed to accept me as I was as well.

Thankfully she did!

When I started my fitness journey, I wasn't expecting to become a more authentic human being. I was not expecting to share my vulnerabilities with the world.

I wasn't expecting these things to happen, but they happened anyway.

I have a long-time client named Polly. Polly is much like you. She has seen some success before, but her mind has always been the thing that's gotten in the way. It seems like no matter what, she'll sabotage her results. Soon after she begins to get them, she will commit to doing something for two weeks, see some progress, see some success, and then it all comes crashing down. She has been through this cycle countless times.

Right now, things are different for Polly. She's gone through a mental and emotional shift. While she's still in her weight loss journey, she is now more accepting of herself. She is now more authentic in her interactions with those around her. Which was often uncomfortable to her.

Polly is not blowing up the charts with results, but her results are steady. What she has accomplished so far is sustainable.

Her constant battle is comparison and compromise.

Polly is thrilled with every change that she sees in her life. She celebrates where she is, even though she is not physically where she is ready to be yet. Perhaps in the next book I'll be able to tell the complete story of her weight loss success. But for now, she's making the changes she needs to in order to live a life she loves. And like you, she's in the midst of her journey.

You may be looking for a physical change, but don't be surprised if you start experiencing a mental and emotional shift as well.

CHAPTER FIVE

How Ten Cows Can Help You Love Yourself

In order to succeed on your weight loss journey, you'll need to be one thing first and foremost: adaptable.

You need to agree that being a person of change and being a person that can overcome obstacles is something that is a part of your DNA. You are the type of person that pushes through. And if you're not that person right now, you will be by the time you finish this book.

Even when it's tough, you'll be the type of person that keeps tough commitments. And you'll be the type of person that even when things don't go your way, you'll keep trying.

What I don't want you to do is to try new things, stick with them for a little while, and then when things start to get hard to quit.

I don't want that for you because I know where that place takes you. It creates a mentality where you're unable to cope, where you can't do it, where you are not fit to do it yourself and you believe that someone else should be the one to do it for you. And in that mindset, you'll be searching for someone else to do it for you. You will look for someone else to give you the perfect plan. You will look for someone else to give you the motivation that you so desperately need. And what you'll find is those things can be given to you, but they cannot be absorbed by you for very long.

Ever hear the phrase "You can give a man a fish and feed him for a day. If you teach a man to fish, you can feed him for a lifetime."

That's what this book is. I'm teaching you to 'fish'.

If all you are ever given is the answer to the question, you will not know how to figure it out on your own. If someone keeps handing you a meal plan you blindly follow what happens when they stop handing you the meal plan?

Right now, you are embarking on an entirely new journey.

From now on, when it comes to your health and fitness, there was the time before this book, and the time after it.

This new journey is at high risk right now.

The first few days and weeks are the highest risk for you to drop out and stop following through. There are going to be innumerable obstacles that get in your way. It will be your job to overcome them.

The more difficult the obstacle, the sweeter your reward will be.

Often when I interview a client that has gotten to their major weight loss goal, they inevitably cry. We see the same thing happen in sports. When great effort is put forth the reward at the end is that much more powerful. They go hand in hand.

Think of it this way.

How valuable is something that you spent a year of hard work trying to get?

How valuable is something that you spent one month trying to get?

Often the crash diets and the short cuts that we take get us the result or most of the result we were hoping for. Quick crash diets can drop pounds in a hurry. But the reward at the end isn't as sweet or satisfying.

Where if we work for longer, in a more focused and methodical manner we can be overwhelmed by the emotion of joy we feel when we get to our destination. That emotion is more powerful because we earned it. Fair and square. No cheating. No short cuts. We did the work. Now we earn the prize.

And because it feels so much more valuable, we treat it that way.

There's an old proverb about a *Ten Cow Wife*. Now before you beat me up, hear me out. This is about a man and a woman back when livestock was traded in exchange for marriage.

A woman came of age. She was rather plain, not particularly smart or gifted, and with nothing hinting that she was anything special. A wealthy suitor came by and offered to pay her father a dowry. The father, seeing that she was rather plain was not expecting much and was willing to settle for almost anything. The typical dowry of the time was one, two, or three cows. Four cows would mean the woman would make an exceptional bride.

The man, known to be a shrewd negotiator, offered the father ten cows, which was unheard of. The father could not believe his luck and agreed before the suitor realized what he was getting and backed out. The two were married that very day. They left the village for another island to spend their first year together.

The next year, the pair returned to the village. The man looked about the same, but the woman was totally unrecognizable. She was donned head to toe in the finest garments and jewelry. Her face was more beautiful, her hair was more vibrant, and her personality and kindness came through in every interaction she had.

The village was in disbelief. They were convinced that it must have been a different woman. Her husband boasted that he knew what he was getting when he paid ten cows for his bride.

This story highlights what most people miss: give someone a reputation to live up to.

While this story references a man giving his wife a reputation to live up to, it's possible to do this for yourself. If you work hard on yourself and will want to be the type of person that lives up to that type of lifestyle and commitment.

I mentioned earlier that there would be tough times ahead. When things get hard, most people rely on willpower to fight their way through it.

That tactic is why most people fail.

If you're playing the willpower game, you have already lost.

A question I often hear is: "Andrew, how can I get stronger willpower?"

And the answer to that is to use your willpower, to flex your willpower. Scientists have found that willpower functions just like a muscle. We can strengthen it, and it will improve, and it will get stronger.

However, also like a muscle. When we use our willpower in the short term, our strength declines. You've probably felt this after a workout. After a hard workout, your muscles feel tired and drained, like you're not even half the power you used to be. It's only after you've had time to rest and recover that you're able to do it again.

Willpower works that same way. Over the course of a day, your willpower is drained.

When someone cuts you off in traffic and you have some choice words, but you choose not to say them. You've used some willpower.

When your boss gives you an assignment that you know is silly, but you do it anyway. You've exercised willpower.

When you want a cookie, a piece of chocolate or a bag of chips, but you say to yourself, I'm on a diet, I'm not going to have it. You have exercised willpower.

Over the course of a day, we exercise a lot of our willpower. It's usually at the end of the day that we find our willpower fails us. We find that in our homes, we are troubled with willpower decisions. And eventually we succumb.

If you play the willpower game, you will lose.

I had a client named Emma. Emma struggled with ice cream. When it's in my house, I also struggle with ice cream. Emma found she kept eating ice cream at night, no matter what she did, she just couldn't resist the temptation to have a scoop. After talking we decided that the best course of action wasn't to give up ice cream forever, although that was her initial thought.

What we decided to do was move the ice cream from the indoor freezer to the outdoor freezer. The outdoor freezer was located a mere 20 feet from the house, but it was outside in the cold. For Emma, this made it so the temptation of ice cream also came with some discomfort. If she wanted to get her ice cream, she would need to brave the cold. And sometimes the cold was very much worth it, but more often than not, Emma chose not to go.

Another side effect was that Emma wasn't continually reminded of ice cream. Every time she opened her indoor freezer, it wasn't there to spark the craving. Emma had created distance. Emma found a way to beat willpower. Willpower was a losing battle for Emma, but by adjusting her environment and by adapting to a changing condition, she found a way to win.

CHAPTER SIX

The One Thing You'll Need to Do to Succeed

I want you to agree right here and right now that things are going to be different. I want you to commit to something.

If I could only give you one tool to get you to your weight loss destination, it would be this:

BE ADAPTABLE.

You are going to be the Swiss Army Knife of people. You will have a tool ready to go for any situation and you'll be trained to use it. Adaptability is going to be something you're known for.

If there's only one takeaway that you get from this entire book is that in order to see and reach your ultimate level of success, you are going to need to make changes along the way.

Have you ever heard the phrase "What got you here, won't get you there"? I recognize, as I'm sure you have, that the things that have brought me to the here and now, may not be the things that get me to my beautiful future.

I need you to promise me right here, right now, that you will be adaptable. Say it out loud. I am adaptable. I will overcome. Success is inevitable.

I AM ADAPTABLE.

One thing you need to watch out for is the first obstacle that comes your way, because the way you deal with that obstacle says a lot about your future success. When things get hard, do you still find a way, or do you quit?

I can remember when I started my journey, one thing I implemented that actually made an enormous difference was making smoothies every day. It's a great way for me to get some extra fiber and nutrients, as well as some good protein in a filling way. Now I'm not some smoothie junkie who is taking a film crew on a world tour introducing people to the power of blended vegetables. I like them, but they aren't the only tool in my toolkit.

Anyway, at the time I was waking up at 4:00AM to get to work. And my 'roommates' at the time, my parents, would not have been happy with me making smoothies that early as their bedroom was very close to the kitchen. The easy route would be, "Well, I guess, smoothies aren't going to happen". But I decided that I was going to make them anyway. I made them the night before and turned that into a part of my bedtime routine.

Before I went to bed, I knew I had to make my smoothies. The way I made it happen was simple. If I didn't make my smoothies, I didn't get to have my smoothies. And when I got to work without smoothies, I had a much more uncomfortable and hungry day. I allowed myself to sit in that level of hunger and discomfort and it didn't take me long to make sure I made smoothies for myself every single day.

There's a speech that we play to our clients quite often. It's by the founder of Primerica, Art Williams. It's called the, *Just Do It* speech. This speech is dynamite. It's no surprise that the next year Nike made that their slogan, although Nike claims it had nothing to do with the speech. At one point during the speech, Art rants about how many people are afraid to follow through on their commitments.

"I'm going to sell my house." He says, pretending to be someone else.

To which Art Williams replies as himself "Wonderful. Just do it."

In a halting comeback he says, "But houses ain't selling."

"Well do it anyway." Much to the crowds delight he picks on a characteristic in all of us that we know is holding us back.

It is easy to be a victim of circumstance. There are always things in motion bigger than we can control. But that doesn't mean we can't adapt, overcome, and "Do it anyway". Even if things aren't going right, even if the situation seems outside of your control, there is something within your power.

If your house is not selling the conventional way, perhaps you need to find a new way to sell it.

If your weight loss isn't happening the way you'd like it to, maybe you need to find a new solution.

You need to "Do it anyway", despite all the voices and the critics you have in your own head.

It's time for a quick win. I want you to think through what is probably going to happen when you start to make changes in your life. What is going to go wrong?

Seriously, take a minute. Start thinking about what's going to go wrong when you start eating better. When you start exercising more regularly and when you start losing weight again, think: what is going to get in my way?

What we're doing right now is anticipating. There is a difference between anticipating and worrying. A huge difference. I hate worrying. It involves thinking without action. Anticipating on the other hand, requires that you take the potential problem you have thought of, and find a way around it or through it.

Have you ever noticed that it's the same problems that get you derailed over and over again?

Maybe it's your spouse not being supportive.

Maybe it's your coworkers undermining your diet.

Or maybe it's your own mental processes that keep you from getting the results you need.

Think of what your obstacles are and plan out how to overcome those obstacles before they stop you again.

Have you ever had an important appointment that you had to get to or a meeting that you just couldn't miss? Was it early in the morning? If so, you may have run the risk of sleeping too late. I've been in this situation before and I have overslept too. What I've learned, is that I need to set two alarms when there's something important. That fateful day, where I had an important meeting to get to the power went out overnight. And the alarm reset itself. Your cell phone may have died overnight. Do you have a second alarm ready to go? That type of preparedness is what's going to get you through the days, weeks, months, and years ahead on your journey.

It may not be the alarm that needs to be foolproof.

Here's a quick list of common, but often unthought of, obstacles to weight loss success:

- Having clean workout clothes ready to go.
- Preparing a grocery shopping list.
- Keeping your exercise area clean and ready for an instant workout.
- Not having healthy food prepared and ready to eat after you buy it.
- Not being on the same page as your significant other.
- Knowing how to work around your injuries.
- Letting a little treat turn into way more.

CHAPTER SEVEN

Why Car Breakdowns in Ethiopia Prove You Can't Outsource Your Weight Loss

I want you to think about your biggest obstacles to weight loss.

Whenever I ask my clients this question, it doesn't take them very long to come up with a short list of what is getting in their way. I'm sure you could do the same. If you're struggling with this, think about what keeps you from losing weight.

Why aren't you at your goal weight right now?

The answers to these questions will be your key to success. You've already identified what is in your way, you know what you're going to need to go through and overcome to get where you need to go. Don't be overwhelmed. Often, the things that you just listed are some of the most difficult things to do. It may be relational based. It may be overcoming a phobia or fear. It may involve something that makes you deeply uncomfortable.

We're not going to tackle these obstacles just yet, but understand that eventually we will, and you will be better for it. I want to prove to you that this is something that you can handle. That this is something you can do, that you are indeed an adaptable person, and you can find a way through these nuanced and difficult obstacles every single day.

Most Americans, at least in the area where I live, drive cars. They get in their cars and they go to their destination. When a person is driving, eventually it becomes instinctual. At first it is far from instinctual, as my mother's panicked gasps and my father's deeply furrowed brow reminded me on my first few times sitting in the driver's seat. On my first left turn I almost took someone out. I can still see the panicked look on my mom's face. Eventually I got the hang of it and eventually it became second nature. Now, if I come across a roadblock, encounter crazy drivers, there's a detour, a speed trap or debris in the road, I have a method that I follow to get me through.

And if I don't have a method, I figure it out. As I go, particularly with detours or things that are immediately blocking the way my creativity comes to life. And I must find a way to go, do I follow the detour signs, or do I rely on my knowledge of the area to get me to where I need to go? Either way I'm overcoming the obstacle one way, maybe a little quicker and one way, maybe a bit slower. Regardless, I'm still going to get to my destination.

Just because there was an obstacle in the road did not mean I stopped my car, turned around, and went home. I still got to my destination. When we're driving, it's unconscious behavior for us to adapt to the changing conditions. We often do it automatically. And when we need to be conscious of it, we take the practiced steps in a new way to get to where we need to go.

You have somewhere you need to go. You need to lose weight. That is the destination. When an obstacle appears, will you just turn around and go home?

There are going to be hardships. There will be challenges, but you are going to adapt to the terrain because you have somewhere to go. You have a destination and you will not be stopped. You may be delayed, detoured, and dang frustrated, but you will not be stopped.

Recently there's been a lot of construction near my house. They're putting a new development in and that development is absolutely gigantic. It is several hundred acres and I'm sure there's going to be tons of apartments and houses built there in the coming months and years. As of right now, they've been laying a lot of the groundwork and that involves tearing up the road. In tearing up the road, I have needed to adapt often. When I pull out of my driveway, I turn a particular direction and a turn, or two later, I come to an intersection where the construction is concentrated. Some days I've needed to turn an entirely different direction as I leave my driveway so that I can avoid the construction delays.

It was hard at first and many times I forgot and paid the ultimate price: I was delayed a few minutes. All kidding aside, it was an inconvenience but eventually I formed a new habit. And ironically, it was just in time to get back into my old habit because they had finished construction.

That is a microcosm of what your weight loss journey is going to look like. There's going to be something that gets in your way.

You will have to adapt.

You're going to make mistakes.

It's not going to go well sometimes, but you're going to need to do it anyway.

It's easy to shoot down this idea. It's easy to opt out of being adaptable. It's easy to be the victim. So often people will tell me that their biggest obstacle is outside of their control.

"It's my husband."

"It's my boss."

"It's my schedule."

"It's because I was abducted by aliens when I was younger and forced to eat cake all day."

I've never actually heard that last one, but I'm sure I will if I stay in the game long enough.

My point is, it's easy to point fingers. You humbly recognize that you are not all powerful. Thus, you cannot control the people around you, which is fair. However, you do have control over yourself and you do have *influence* on those around you. While many things are not under your direct control, you do have the ability to improve the situation.

Martha Beck, author of the book *The Four Day Win*, has great ideas on how to improve a situation. She recommends to better it, barter it, or bag it. And while her terminology is unique to her, the technique is not exactly new.

There are many ways to go about solving a problem. One problem that I have: dishes. The bane of my domestic life, dishes are the hot and smelly gateway to a past nightmare. I used to work as a dishwasher in my teenage years and since then, I feel like I've washed my share of dishes for a lifetime. Dishes are not a joy for me.

However, I have found a way to make doing dishes better. I have incorporated growth and learning time into my dish time. I made a deal with my wife. Whenever I'm doing dishes, I listen to an audio book or a podcast. This for me, makes the dish washing more palatable. And it feels less like a chore and more like an opportunity for me to improve and to get better. This is my way of BETTERING my dishwashing.

There are other ways to overcome or compromise with tough problems. One thing that many do is outsource. By giving something that you don't want to do to someone else, you are BARTERING. In a free market economy this typically involves and transfer of money for service or work rendered. I do this all the time with my car. I don't have a garage or the tools necessary to make most work on my car go smoothly. I tend to hire a mechanic to fix things. But I do so at my own peril.

I have a friend who did a lot of missionary work in Ethiopia. Cars are a little bit rarer there and the roads are significantly bumpier. Couple that with the long roads in the literal middle of nowhere and it makes knowing how to repair a car a necessity.

On your weight loss journey, that logic applies to you as well. You won't be successful if you just outsource your problem (excess weight) to someone else. You need to learn how to actually solve it on your own.

I am putting myself at risk by not knowing how to take care of my car effectively. Are you willing to put your body at risk because you don't want to learn how to take care of it?

If you just can't find a way to make the problem better or a way to outsource it, then perhaps it's time to try BAGGING it. This may mean you drop something entirely.

I've tried this method with dishwashing, and it doesn't really work. The dishes stay there waiting for me. Or my wife gets fed up and I get a talking to. You'll certainly need to be strategic in your use of this one, but it may be the best answer.

I can remember when I was attending college at my first school my grades steadily slipped until I finished my sophomore year with a 1.9 GPA for the semester. My dad sat me down and with more concern than anger asked me about my grades. As I talked about my grades, I also started talking about how I didn't like my major, the school, and a lot of the friendships I had made. He cut me to the core with one statement.

"You don't have to stay there, you know. It's your life, you can do whatever you want."

As simple as that was, I had never thought about leaving. I felt like I was already too invested and that to change would mean a total loss of progress. I felt like I needed to stay to see my initial investment through. Gamblers often make this same mistake. It even has a name: The Sunk Cost Fallacy. The Sunk Cost Fallacy is the belief that you've already invested so much, it would be a waste not to see it through to the end.

There comes a time when you need to cut your losses and move on.

As soon as my false belief was shattered, I could clearly feel what the right thing to do was. The obvious choice was to leave the school, and if I wanted to continue my education, find a new one. So, I bagged it and moved on. Looking back on my life that is a very distinct turning point where my life may have gone very differently had I continued.

In reading this book and applying its principles you'll discover many false beliefs that have been holding you back. Keep going, you're almost halfway!

CHAPTER EIGHT

What Dave Ramsey, Disney World, and Picking Lettuce Off My Hamburgers Have to Do with Motivation

Many people list their spouse as one of their biggest obstacles to weight loss. This can be extremely difficult because your spouse is not under your direct control. And often when we get excited about a new nutritional plan or a new exercise routine, we want to share that with those that are closest to us. And if we've done that too many times and haven't gotten the results that were promised often, those who are closest to us also feel the most burned by it.

If you're going to your spouse and telling him or her, "Hey, I've got this new diet plan or this new eating routine we're going to be getting into it involves us eating nothing that we like. It's going to be very uncomfortable and you're going to be grumpy most of the time. Isn't that exciting?"

Your spouses' most likely response is going to be a resounding "NO".

So, what do you do? Dave Ramsey, a financial coach and radio host sees this situation arise often as people get motivated to transform their finances. People who are looking to make a financial change need to get their important people around them on board. And often they follow a similar approach to what I just described. Many of the things Ramsey prescribes are radical, uncomfortable, and counter cultural. It may involve selling off expensive cars, eating beans and rice, and drastically cutting extra expenditures.

It comes as no surprise that money quickly becomes a battleground when the changes proposed are so drastic. What Ramsey recommends is to start with a beautiful picture of the future. We've worked through the Baby Steps Ramsey proposes and have seen incredible peace in our finances, even in times of financial difficulty. At first, my wife and I were not on the same page financially. It took me connecting with something that she loves and building a future towards that for her to fully engage with the plan.

One thing that resonates with my wife Samantha is visits to Disney world. For me, a trip to Disney world when our kids are very small is not that important because they will most likely forget almost all of it. What I would rather see is multiple trips when they're a little bit older. And so right now, our bargain is this: we are going to save and work hard now, so that in the future, we are able to go to Disney world more often.

And that may be the tactic you take with your spouse. You show them the beautiful future, where you're both healthier, where you're able to do more, where you're both vibrant and feel younger and less crabby than you do now. And that beautiful future is worth making short term sacrifices for one another.

While some people cite their spouse as their biggest obstacle, others claim that they are just not creative or gifted in the areas required to do well at health and fitness.

To this, I must call baloney. Often the reason you don't feel creative or the reason you don't feel like you're the type of person that's able to do that is because when you do that thing, you feel powerless or weak or trapped, or it frustrates you beyond all measure. All you really want is the problem solved and you just don't have the mental energy to work on it right now.

I have a client who, every time she encounters a problem with technology throws her arms up in the air and says, "I'm just not tech savvy. This is just always the way that it goes with me. Every time I interact with technology, it's just too hard and it just doesn't work." This way of thinking is called a fixed mindset.

I've worked with many people in her demographic. I can tell you, she has no more and no less problems than those around her. However, her experience with them and the way she has internalized her problem with technology has created a crisis of identity. There are people that are good with technology, and there are those that are not. She has planted herself firmly in the latter category.

When things are hard it is easy to take the mental shortcut of black and white. You're good at it or you're not. You're talented or you're not. But the world is made up of gray areas, with very few pure binary choices. That gray area is more of a sliding scale of skill, experience, and outlook. What this individual struggles with is not technology, it's the belief that she is not good with technology. That seed was planted long ago by an incident that she can probably still remember that rears itself up to haunt her every time she struggles in that realm.

Memories like that are baggage. You're welcome to carry it around for as long as you like. But the fastest way forward is to drop your baggage and run free. The memories that have taught us that things are impossible or that we are not enough or that we are not capable are the most detrimental memories that we have. They box us into a reality that attempts to justify the wrongdoings of the past. It is only by stepping beyond the box we've created that we can get results at a level we never have before.

Whether you're a technophobe, convinced you lack creativity, or you think you're just not a good cook, you will do whatever it takes to prove that belief. Humans are remarkable in that respect. We have a strong pull to be consistent and to create a persistent world view that justifies our beliefs and the way we live. If you believe you are not creative you will struggle with writer's block, avoid art like the plague, and seek ways to prove yourself right. Each small step forward into new territory is stressful and at the first sign of trouble your automatic response will be "See, I'm no good at _____." As if a minor setback proves an incorrect theory.

We're going to break a false belief, are you ready?

I want you to think of something that you are just not good at. Think of a skill or ability that just never materialized for you. Swimming, dancing, public speaking, telling jokes, cooking, being vulnerable, being healthy, having coordination, singing, and handling technology are all common areas that people feel inadequate and often harbor false beliefs about their true ability.

Pick your thing that you're convinced you have no aptitude at.

Imagine what you would feel like if you were able to do that thing well.

If you struggle with cooking, imagine what it would be like to cook a meal that was pleasing to your family. Bask in the glow of the compliments they give you as they eat your wonderfully prepared food.

Now imagine someone that you know who is good at the thing you feel you are not so good at. I don't want you to pick someone who is exceptional, just someone who is merely good. Try and pick someone who is nearby in demographics to you. Someone you would consider a peer.

Did this individual come out of the womb with some special talent for cooking? Or did they try cooking on their own and get better at it over time? The reason I had you pick someone who is good at something versus someone who excels at it is simple: the gulf between poor performance and excellence is huge. The difference between poor performance and good performance is considerably smaller.

I want you to imagine this friend at the age of 2. Imagine them doing the skill you wish to have at age two with the same skill they have now. Seems ridiculous right? Picturing a two-year-old swimming laps in the pool or imagining them climbing up on high chairs to cook a meal seems a bit absurd. And It highlights an important fact: they were not born with this talent. They developed it over time.

I want you to think of the memory or memories that prove your theory that you are just no good at _____.

Often it involves external or internal judgement. There is a high-pressure situation that we perceive we have failed at. Sometimes publicly sometimes all by ourselves. But that failure proves to us that we can't do it.

Imagine now, that right at that moment of despair, a mentor stepped in. Right now, that mentor is you. You step in and say the opposite of whatever is ringing through the mind of your past self. If your past self is convinced that you'll never be any good at sports, tell that younger version of you that it just takes more practice.

Do you know what separates a high school band teacher from a musician in a symphony orchestra?

It's not natural talent. It is time spent on focused practice. If you could tally up the number of hours spent in focused practice on a particular instrument the deviation between good musicians and great ones becomes obvious. The great ones put in thousands more hours of practice by the same point in their lives.

That is all that separates you from what you perceive as impossible. In performance art the differences are measured in the thousands of hours. But often in our own lives and the things that we want to be better at, the difference is measured in the tens or at most, hundreds of hours. Just a little bit more focused practice can yield tremendous benefits in the way you go about your everyday life.

Think about something you are particularly skilled at. There is something I promise you. Maybe it's your cooking, the way you do your makeup, the way that you wrap presents, the way you drive, or how you take care of your garden. In all of these things you started off worse than you are right now. You have improved and honed these skills over time.

I can't tell you how many times my wife has run out of a particular type of makeup that she needs yet finds a way to still do her makeup so that she looks fabulous. It helps that I think she looks fabulous without it, but the point remains. She adapts and overcomes and finds a way to make things nice.

You have all sorts of false beliefs. Some of them are helping you, and some of them are crippling you. More than likely, some of your beliefs are doing both. Whether you feel like you're not creative, you're not a vegetable person, or you're just not capable of losing weight, deep down these things don't have to be true. You choose for them to be true.

Years ago, when I was overweight and depressed, I considered myself a carnivore, as well as a beer drinker. I was never a vegetable guy. I went to the point of picking off the lettuce and the tomatoes from my hamburgers. It was extreme. I avoided greens and vegetables at all costs. And then somewhere in my journey, I decided I'd give them a shot. I tested it.

I asked myself, well, it was true at one point, is it still true now?

And what I found was they weren't all that great, but I decided to keep going anyway. Remember do the thing anyway? So, I did it. I tried making them all kinds of different ways. I stumbled upon green smoothies and I loved them. Not at first though. My first green smoothie was actually a milkshake. And I put in a couple of leaves of spinach. It was quite delicious, but the chunks of spinach seemed to get in the way of it. Years later, I can look back on that smoothie with a chuckle because now they are packed to the gills with wonderful greens and make a big impact in my nutrition. However, at one point I would have looked at that green smoothie and said, yeah, no thanks, hard pass.

My distaste for vegetables was so extreme that when my mom found out I was eating vegetables regularly, she got tears in her eyes and almost wept. I almost made my mom cry because I finally ate vegetables.

Don't be afraid to test your beliefs. Don't be afraid to put them out to pasture. If it's time for them to go, I've done it and you can do it too. The right beliefs will stay with you and stand up to the test of time. The wrong ones will weed themselves out, if you take the time to prune them.

CHAPTER NINE

You May Accidentally Become a Hero

There will be a lot of changes that happen as you lose weight. One that you may not realize is that you will come to love your life again. It's a bold claim to assert, I know. Even if you feel like things are good now, you may not even realize how much better it will get.

I almost didn't even realize that I had stopped loving my life until I started loving it again. It's taken me some time to figure out when I feel my best. But it is often correlated with looking my best. It's when I'm sleeping well, and my clothes fit perfectly. I feel my best when I'm accomplishing and achieving. I feel my best when I'm making a difference. I'm at my best when I'm connecting well with people that I care about. Each one of these things was improved when I got in better shape and I know you'll experience the same benefits.

If you have that perpetual cloud of extra weight on your body, it becomes a worry. Doctor's appointments become stressful occasions. Clothes shopping becomes an exercise in futility. Sometimes you wonder if people are judging you because of it. Sometimes you wonder if you would feel better or look better. It becomes easier to try and hide and coast. To stop living a full life because it would draw too much attention to you. Attention means that people will see you and being seen starts to become the scariest thing of all.

I can remember my initial cause for exercise was a little bit vain. I wanted to look good. And in particular, I wanted to look good for the ladies. What I found though, was looking good was only part of the battle. I needed to be good person. I needed to connect well. And I needed to commit myself to something bigger than me.

What I found was looks were certainly not everything. For me being in shape gave me confidence and that confidence was extremely helpful. That confidence was ultimately what led me to my bride and the confidence to start a life together. You may be well past these motivations, and that's okay. While confidence is wonderful, there's a few other traits that are even more beneficial.

When you take care of yourself you will have a level of competence and understanding of your capabilities. These traits often go unnoticed, until you really wish you had them.

A client of mine, Karin was going for a walk with some friends who were visiting from out of state. While they were walking, they came across a scenario that sounds like it came straight out of a first aid handbook. They came across a lady who was having severe back pain. She was laying down and was unable to get up off of the trail. This was a situation that could get sticky in a hurry.

Karin, who happens to be a nurse, performed wonderfully. The trail was isolated and a bit remote so it would be a long haul to help this woman to a spot where she could get into a vehicle. Karin's friends weren't all that confident. As a matter of fact, they weren't all that capable, either. They were out of shape and they had a laundry list of their own ailments and excuses that kept them from helping. It was up to Karin and the husband to help carry this woman to where she needed to get to.

Karin had the capability. Karin had the confidence and Karin knew that she could help. Think about what it would feel like to be one of

Karin's friends, looking on. What emotions may have been playing through their minds? Were they embarrassed? Sad? Wishful?

Think about Karin, what was Karin feeling? Nervous? Confident? Empowered?

Karin was helping. She was using something that she never thought she would use. She was using her strength as an opportunity to help someone. We often don't realize the opportunities that we miss out on because we are out of shape or carrying around extra weight. These opportunities pass us by every day, but it is a great detriment to the world around us. You recognize what that feeling is like to look on from the sidelines, wishing that you could be of more help. You want things to be better. You're working on taking care of your condition. When the time comes for you to be a hero, you'll be ready.

The best thing you can do right now is to keep reading, keep going, keep on this journey.

CHAPTER TEN

What's Really Wrong with the Weight Loss Industry

The biggest mistake that people make is outsourcing their brains. When you outsource your brain, you allow someone else to take charge of your body. And when someone else is in charge of your body, they may do things better. But what happens when you regain control of your brain? If you didn't take the time to learn and to grow and to change your brain, your brain is the same as it was. And guess what? Your brain will see and do the same things that it used to. If you have outsourced your brain to a diet or a fad you have put your body in someone else's hands. And in the short term, you may see some wonderful results. But eventually you will regain control of your body. Your brain will come back. And if your brain has not adapted to your new body, your brain will bring you back to your old body.

One of the worst examples of this is a crash diet. I've seen these advertised all over the place sometimes by people that have doctor-like credentials. And it is so frustrating because I know what's going to happen to these poor souls who get trapped by fancy marketing and trustworthy credentials. They're going to see incredible results in the short term. And after a while of hardship, they're going to get back into their normal routine. And less than a few years later, there'll be in the same spot that they were when they started, except along the way, they will have lost some muscle. And in losing some of that muscle, everything else becomes more difficult to do.

I was talking to one of my clients the other day and she was extremely distraught after a blood test showed that she needed to go on medications that she had hoped to avoid. As she talked through her feelings, she said "I'm just going to stop eating, that's the only thing that's ever worked."

My heart broke and my anger boiled. I felt for her situation. She was so desperate for results that she was willing to do anything, *anything*, to get them. I felt a righteous anger rising in me because she had been so twisted by the diet industry that she truly believed the only path to results was starvation. The marketing and media messages she had received over the years were so numerous and contradictory that her conclusion was a dismal one.

As I told my client, starvation is not an option. For both mental and physical reasons. On the physical side, muscle is like an extra calorie burn just for being alive. It's like passive income for your calories. In financial terms passive income is the holy grail: get paid without working. Within your body, muscle acts the same way, you burn more calories just by existing. When we are extremely calorie restricted, our bodies will make the easy choice of destroying the inefficient muscle we've created to both use as fuel and to improve our overall fuel efficiency.

Something you may not be aware of is that muscle is hard to come by. Our body is ruthlessly efficient and will do whatever it takes to survive. That efficiency is a detriment to our muscle unless we convince our body that we need it. The best way to convince your body you need muscle? You guessed it – exercise! Particularly strength training.

So, if we are systematically killing off our muscle through crash dieting, we are in a sense cutting off our possibilities of a restful and easy future. It's like pilfering your retirement fund so you can buy a nicer house. You are signing yourself up for tons and tons of extra work on the back end. Yuck. Again, be careful of what you sign yourself up for. If you decide to follow a diet plan or a weight loss program that is spoon-feeding you an exact step by step formula to follow, you will eventually fail because they're going to go out of business or you may move on, or you may have a falling out with this individual or business. In the aftermath of leaving that program you're left with what you used to do. And what you used to do got you to where you are right now.

Shortcuts can be so seductive. We become convinced that we can have the thing for a fraction of the cost and reap the full benefit. I saw this when I was in college. Many students cheated their way through school. They looked up the answers or got the answer sheet and found ways to memorize it. And then after they had passed the tests, after they got their degrees, they wondered why it was difficult for them to get a job or keep a job. They had cheated their way through school. They had gotten the qualification, but the qualification was hollow. It didn't actually provide what they thought it would. It got them a foot in the door, but it didn't keep them in the building. Eventually they were kicked out. They struggled because they didn't have the skills they claimed they did. That is what happens when we follow a plan that someone else has created for us and we don't come up with anything on our own.

When we do that, we are setting ourselves up to have the necessary credentials, but not to have the skills to maintain that position. Your credentials will be weight loss. You may lose the weight, but you don't have the expertise to keep that weight off. And so, what happens is eventually you are exposed. Eventually it's found out and eventually that weight comes to find you again. I don't want you to go through that cycle again. Often my clients have gone through that cycle numerous times, many upwards of five times. By working with me, I want this to be your last time on the way down. This is your last time to the bottom, and we are going to maintain it from there.

I had a client named Kevin. In his first year made some awesome progress. When we first started working together Kevin lost almost 30 pounds. And in doing so felt great, but he was ready for more results. And then bam, COVID hit. And boy was that tough. We ended up not seeing each other and working together for the better part of a year. And over the course of that year, he gained back all that he had lost. When I started working with Kevin again, Kevin was ready to hop back on where'd he left off. Kevin was looking for someone else to make the meals for him. Kevin was busy. Kevin had a lot going on, but if Kevin wanted to see success in the future, he was going to need to adapt and to change. Kevin needs to learn and grow just like you.

Now, you can try and do this learning all on your own. Many have and have found great success doing that. What I've seen is that going alone takes significantly longer and oftentimes you'll fall into someone else's web and they will spin you a tale and get you on their plan. And then you'll end up back where you started.

Another issue you'll run into when you go at it alone is knowing who to trust. After the end of World War II, many Japanese soldiers continued terrorizing the islands that they had been stationed on. There were some cases where a Japanese soldier had lived on an Island for more than 20 years, continuing a guerrilla campaign and living off the land. These soldiers were called Japanese holdouts and the last one that surrendered did so in 1974, a staggering 28 years after Japan had formally surrendered.

We can look on as outsiders and see that it's a little crazy for these soldiers to carry on this way in the face of overwhelming evidence that should have convinced them to change. I see this same dogged determination when it comes to fitness and health on the general population as well as with some of my clients.

They were dialed in to what they had to do, but they weren't absorbing the new information that was coming in. They weren't able to adapt to a change in the world around them. This is often what happens when we do it alone. If you go alone, you may find a solution that works for you. However, that solution may eventually become outdated, outmoded, and become obsolete. And what will you do when that happens? You've spent enough time being lost in the woods, and you've probably spent more than enough time waiting for change to find you. How often have you continued on, blindly hoping that the stars would line up just right, so that things could start working again.

I see this most often when people step on the scale, they'll step on the scale, throw their arms up in disbelief and say, "Well, why aren't things working?"

And my first question is usually, are you doing anything different or new?

And their response is no, almost incredulous that I would ask such a silly question and that underlines why they aren't seeing any progress. If you have hit a plateau and you haven't seen weight loss using the tactics you are used to, you more than likely will need some new inputs and ideas. Your way of doing things has gotten you to this point. Now you'll need to tweak, test and adjust the way you do things to get different results going forward. Notice how I didn't say "Your plan got you here, now you need to do my plan to get to the next step."

That is exactly the kind of thinking I'm advocating against. I'm helping you throw spaghetti at the wall to see what sticks for you, so you can make it a regular part of your life. I am not going to cook your dinner for you and tell you what to eat.

On the flip side, doing the same things and hoping that your body will change is a losing strategy as well.

Often it is your own words and way of thinking that will keep you stuck.

One phrase I hear a lot is "I'll try to..." and you can fill in the blank.

"I'll try to lose weight."

"I'll try to log my food."

"I'll try to make a grocery list."

"I'll try to show up to my workouts."

And then do you know what happens?

Nothing. The person committed to "trying" doesn't get it done. But I could have told them they weren't going to do it right when they said that.

A wise old sage named Yoda once said "Do or do not. There is no try."

If you've been trying to lose weight, listen up.

Stop trying. Change the language you use. Trying is an adult's way of saying "I want something but am not going to put in the work to do it." We shy away from commitment because it stings when we don't follow through.

Start saying "I will" and your results will begin to show up.

And if they don't, you'll get to have the sting that comes with not upholding a commitment. Which is actually a good thing. Most people consider themselves people of honestly and integrity. And we love to be congruent. We mean what we say, and we do what we promise.

It's why a stray phrase from early in a politician's career can be their undoing. If they are seen as "flip floppers" they quickly lose trust in the eyes of the public.

We want to mean what we say. That little sting that comes with not following through, while uncomfortable, can help push us in the right direction. Small disappointments lead to big breakthroughs.

What you don't want is what comes when you don't get those small little stings. When you avoid them, you end up getting a huge sting later. Your doctor starts talking to you about bad news in a hushed tone. You step on the scale and see a number you never imagined. You put on your favorite outfit and find that it no longer fits.

Those moments are big stings, and they feel awful. You want the small stings sooner rather than later that way you can avoid the big stings that mean you're in deep trouble.

And it starts with language. The way you describe what you are going to do will help to frame your mind and get you accountable to the work you're doing.

CHAPTER ELEVEN

"Who Keeps Destroying My Wall?!"

In order for you to succeed you'll need to make a routine out of forecasting and adjusting. At some point, all things go wrong. Systems will fail. Problems will come up and you will need to find a solution. If you've done a good job forecasting, you will have already anticipated most of the punches that life is going to throw at you. And if you already anticipated what those punches are going to be, you're already blocking and dodging or at the very least covering up. So, you're not hit quite as hard or as unexpectedly.

The process of forecasting sounds like it's time intensive. There are entire professions dedicated to it. One that pops to mind is that of the weather person. They spend all of their time analyzing and modeling. And then tell us what they've come up with. You may think that forecasting takes too much time. That it takes too long to try and think about the future. You may think that spending all that time preparing for something that might never happen means you wasted that prep time.

Imagine the military of the United States. Individual soldiers work together to achieve larger objectives. What do they spend most of their time doing? It's not fighting. They spend most of their time preparing. Preparing their equipment and preparing their plan and strategy. They spend time drilling and working on their fitness. Why is that? It's because they don't know exactly how a situation is going to unfold so they prepare for different outcomes, that way when a situation arises, they can come out ahead.

This happens to us every day. Situations come at us. And the less prepared we are, the more likely it is that it doesn't work out in our favor.

Have you ever had a day where it seems like you're always on the defensive? It's like every time you try and do something an unforeseen obstacle pops up. Each time your energy, motivation, and willpower are sapped.

How do you feel at the end of one of those days?

It's usually a 'Dish me up an extra serving and throw some ice cream in there while you're at it' kind of days.

I don't know about you, but I hate those kinds of days. They make me feel entitled and I know they set me back. It'd be nice to have less of those days.

When we're in a reactionary mode, it feels like taking the time to predict and think ahead is going to take time away from actually executing on what we need to do. I want you to imagine that you are a mason and you're building a wall. It's hard work and you spend all week doing it. You don't finish it, but you take some time off for the weekend. Over the weekend, someone comes in and smashes all your work. Now you come back on Monday and you see your wall all smashed up and you must repair your wall before you can even pick up where you left off.

At some point in the week, you get back into your groove and you begin making progress again. The wall gets a little bigger. Before you know it, the weekend has arrived again and it's time to take a break.

You get back on Monday, and lo and behold the wall is smashed up. Again. This time, it's even worse and will take you longer to repair.

You're probably thinking this person should do something about this. Clearly a vandal or your nemesis is coming in to mess up your life. You should put of a fence, hire security, put up a camera, or do something!

What's shocking is that this same thing happens to people every week, for years on end. And they do very little to protect the wall they are trying to build. That wall is like your health. And we spend a lot of time working at it and cultivating it. If you had put up a camera to record who goes near the wall do you know what you'd find? The person vandalizing the wall is the same person who is building it!

If it takes too much time to plan, then we are going to have to deal with the consequences of not planning. And the consequence is often that we must pick up the pieces and get our lives right again before we get back into the groove of making progress.

During the week, most people tend to be on track. There's renewed determination, a schedule, and a routine that keeps things moving forward. And then something happens over the weekend.

You come back on Monday and must pick up the pieces. Often, I see this when people step on the scale on a Monday, or they refuse to step on the scale on a Monday, because they don't want to know the extent of the damage that was done. They don't even want to look at it. They'd rather just start picking up the pieces and just try and start building again.

This insanity is what forecasting and adjusting saves us from. If your wall keeps getting smashed, you should do something to protect it! If you know someone is coming for that wall you can set up a gate.

You can create a barrier. You can use stronger materials. You can find a way to keep your wall from getting smashed, to keep your progress from being deleted so that you don't have to spend half of the following week just catching up to where you used to be.

That's why so much about weight loss seems like two steps forward and three steps back. It feels like whenever you make progress, it is lost just as quickly. It's because we aren't taking the critical time to think ahead and plan for what is coming at us.

You need to guard your progress at all costs. And to do that will take some innovation and ingenuity.

You know this truth deep down: to get somewhere you've never been (or haven't been in a long while) you'll have to do some things you've never done.

Remember Tom, the retired teacher?

One thing that was remarkable about Tom was that he was committed to continually testing and trying new things in order to get new results. He even tried old things in new ways. He would try old meal plans or different styles of additional activity to see if those things worked. Some of them did, and some of them did not, but one thing remained true. Tom was committed to trying. He continually tested and experimented with his body, the grand experimentation device, and his results were awesome.

Tom had numerous bad months and setbacks. But one thing remained: his fascination and willingness to experiment. He tested more in his first year than most people do in a lifetime. Looking at his weight loss over time, it looks like a straight line headed down. But if you were to plot the graph as a pounds lost per month graph; it looks more like a lie detector test. His weight loss was not steady, in the month by month sense. But it was over the course of the year.

If even in the month by month data he was on a roller coaster, what do you think it was like week to week, or day to day?

Do you think Tom pouted and threw in the towel every time the scale went up after he worked hard at it? Certainly not, but he did have plenty of tough days, tough weeks, and tough months. That was why I was so fascinated by him, because so many clients would quit at the first sign of difficulty.

Tom excelled at learning and adapting. Anything he bought, read, watched, or listened to was a means to that end. It wasn't money that was going to get him better, it was knowledge and the skilled application of that knowledge.

There are many ways that you can go about buying your way out of your predicament. You could have a stomach surgery, you could get liposuction, you could have meals delivered to your house. You could hire a personal chef. All of these things are shortcutting the main route. By going with these shortcut devices, you're not going to be able to learn from your experiences. You're taking out the opportunity for you to adjust and to grow and to get better

By buying this book, by reading it, and more importantly, by applying the principles that we've talked about, you're finally going to be in the shape you've always wanted to be. You won't have to fumble with these botched shortcuts that don't work or fall into uncontrolled weight gain ever again.

CHAPTER TWELVE

Why the Nicest Thing I Could Say Was "I Hope I Never See You Again"

Do you want to hear a little secret? When you apply it, you'll be able to see your results stick around for longer. You'll have more motivation, feel more inclined to partake in healthy behaviors, and you'll be able to tell right away that you're making progress.

This one little secret is a keystone habit. A keystone habit helps other healthy habits stay established.

A keystone is the center top piece of an archway. Once the keystone is in place, all the other building material solidifies into one piece. Without the keystone the other building materials would fall apart or at best would be significantly less stable.

A keystone habit is equally as powerful when it comes to building a solid foundation of healthy behaviors.

The king of healthy keystone habits is exercise.

Exercising can become a keystone habit even if it's for just a few minutes a day. The reason exercise functions so well as a keystone habit has to do with some of the consequences of exercise. The main consequence that we recognize on a minute by minute basis is the soreness that we feel after we've done something new and challenging. That soreness works as a subtle reminder. It says, "You've already worked hard on this!"

Reminders are powerful things. We learned about that with Emma and the ice cream. Whenever she opened up the freezer just seeing the ice cream was a subtle reminder in the back of her brain that ice cream was available. And that reminder stuck with her until her willpower was at its weakest.

When you exercise, you will find that you are more motivated. That little bit of soreness is a subtle reminder that brings to mind the sacrifices you've made to get where you are.

When you stand up from your chair to walk into the kitchen, you may be reminded that you've already worked on yourself today and that some of your next decisions should start to align with that work. It's the same reason military discipline works so well. You start by making your bed. Then you move on to the next task and by the time you're through your morning routine you're accomplished and ready for action. Excellence in one area breeds excellence elsewhere.

Your keystone habit of exercise will start to invade other areas of your life. You'll have already taken a step forward in the right direction and you won't want to take a step backwards because you've already worked so hard for that one step.

Don't think that you need to exercise for extraordinary amounts of time in order to still receive this benefit. Even a few minutes, each day and done consistently can bring you that benefit. Over time, you'll start to experience more rewards from the exercise time that you're investing, and you'll be more inclined to do longer workouts. Don't be perfect on day one. Start with a rough plan and take it from there.

You may be extremely tempted right now to flip ahead in the book to say, "Yeah, yeah, yeah, enough talk about strategy and head work, it's time for me to do something!"

I would caution you.

The last few chapters will bring all that you have absorbed so far and turn it into an action plan.

Action plans are vital to long term success. I can remember a client of mine who had joined our live classes, which we call bootcamp, decided to venture out on her own. Her fitness plans for the future were vague at best, but I hoped she would find success in her efforts. I said to her, "I hope I don't see you again."

At first, she was very taken aback. I flashed a genuine and caring smile. And she recognized what that meant. It meant I wished her the best. I wished that the things she learned would become a permanent part of her life. I wanted her to spread her wings and own her fitness destiny. I wanted what she learned to be a piece of her lifestyle.

Unfortunately, I did end up seeing that client again and I work with her occasionally to this day. However, in working with her, she is not a failure. What has happened is she has continued to grow. She has continued to learn, and she has continued to master not only her body, but master her own life as well. She and her husband have ventured out on their own and have started their own business. They are creating the life they have always wanted.

I cannot overstate how important it is to have the right person or the right people in your corner. When I lived in Buffalo it felt like it was dark all the time. I stayed up so late that I tended to sleep away much of the day. The people that I had in my corner cared a lot about me, but they didn't have the expertise or even the self-awareness to take care of themselves. None of cared enough to do what was actually helpful for each other. We all just limped through our lives and used each other to help numb the tough times and find momentary fun instead of seeking a deeper level of satisfaction. It was only when I changed my environment and the inputs in my life that I was able to learn, adjust, and grow into the person I needed to be.

It was my brother, Jeremy taking me under his wing and showing me how to take better care of myself that ultimately ended up changing the trajectory of my life. Not only did it affect my career at first, but it affected my eating too. It affected my mind, and it eventually led to my salvation in Christ.

During my time of personal change and growth I attended church regularly for the first time in my adult life.

Eventually I joined a church group and what I found there was incredible. I found people who were willing to share and who were willing to connect. I was willing to be the first to share and that drastically changed the dynamic of the group. I was willing to be the first to go deep and be vulnerable. And what I found was by going deep and being vulnerable and surrounding myself with the right people, it made the tough times easier and made it so that I could connect with myself from the past. I could recognize and sympathize with that self who had been so left behind and abandoned. It also allowed me to start taking steps, to take care of my current and future self. It allowed me to set up a life that I could be proud of and to live in such a way that I would do my creator proud.

The right people around you are going to inspire you. They are going to encourage you. And they're going to bring you to the next level. I hope at this point, you consider me one of those people. I am in your corner. I care about you. And I want to see you ultimately succeed, not just in your weight loss goal, but with all the goals you have in your life. Weight loss is just a small piece. And my dream for you is that weight loss was just the beginning. I dream that weight loss was the start of a transformation that brought about a change in you. A change so profound that people begin asking what you're doing. They not only say you look healthier, but you are brighter and bring more joy to the world.

CHAPTER THIRTEEN

The Reason Falling Down is a Part of Success

Your biggest obstacle to date has been your own mind. It has been something that has gotten in your way time and time again. Today we are making a change. Today is a day where you look back and remember the decision you made.

Today is where you **quit** and **commit**.

You quit dieting, and you commit to adapting. You quit beating yourself up and you commit to building yourself up. You quit focusing on a big unattainable goal, and you commit to doing the small things every day. It is through quitting that you will find your commitment grow. You need to let go of the things that have gotten you to where you are today. And there are many things that have brought you to where you are today. Many of them are good, but you may need to let go of the good in order to truly embrace the great, because I believe that there's another layer to you.

I believe that there is greatness within you just waiting to leap out and change the world. And I believe that weight loss is just the tip of the iceberg when it comes to your life and what can happen if you commit. What you're going to find is progress.

When you first start out, you have that fire, you have that excitement of something new. Eventually that fire burns out. That initial excitement fades away and all you're left with is the cold, harsh reality that the thing that you want is far away and you are in a difficult situation. That gap that you're in is the hardest gap of all. The gap between the initial excitement and at that first taste of success. When you start off on a weight loss program, oftentimes the quick wins are what is needed to get you the momentum you need to carry on. The plans that I am often recommending don't necessarily contain the immediate quick weight loss. To do that would often take crash dieting, fasting, or doing a cleanse. And these things are short-lived and temporary. They bridge that gap quickly. However, they don't give you that long-lasting fire that will keep your momentum going for the long-term.

Once you can bridge that gap, once you can make it from initial fire to a sustainable fire, once you start seeing results, once people start complimenting you on the changes they see in you, once you experience that high from fitting into a new pair of pants that you thought were too small. Once you experience these moments, you will be hooked, and you will have what it takes to keep going.

Your key is going to be to bridge that gap. You must commit to doing whatever it takes for however long it takes to get that first result. It may take a week. It may take a month. It may take three months. You need to commit to bridging the gap. You're excited right now. You're ready to start right now. And there's a reason I haven't let you go. There's a reason I haven't allowed you to start your journey just yet.

It's because I need you to know that to bridge the gap, to get from that starting fire of excitement to that sustainable burning momentum, there is a cold, dark gap where most people fall and never recover. You must commit to bridging that gap here and now.

Say this out loud:

I AM COMMITTED.

Did you actually say it out loud? If you can't commit to saying three words out loud, what makes you think you can commit to losing the weight?

Say it loud and proud:

I AM COMMITTED.

Much better!

We've already got some momentum rolling now. In the days and weeks ahead, you will not only see progress in your health, but you'll translate that into more productivity. There will be more positivity in your life. Your relationships around you will improve, and you will be unstoppable.

There will be obstacles. There is no doubt about that, but your momentum will carry you through.

There's a wrestler whose story to me is quite fascinating. His name is Diamond Dallas Page or DDP for short. He often played the heel (bad guy) type character within the WWE universe. He was brash, bold, and manly, and he often wore leather and had a moppy blonde mullet which actually looked good even by today's standards. The wrestling sphere is dangerous, occasionally deadly, and certainly painful. At the end of his wrestling career DDP's body was a mess. He had worked out incredibly hard. He had damaged it through his exploits in the ring and from his abuse of it outside of the ring.

He was a broken man. But he committed to something. He committed to getting better, to improving himself, to making his body more flexible, to making his body a temple. And in doing that, he was able to inspire the world, not with his story, but because someone else watched his story unfold, because someone took his story and made it their own.

After DDP had his personal awakening and restored his mobility and ability through yoga, he set out to inspire more people to do the same. He had a student who began his yoga program and began videoing himself. He was a former military combatant and was left with some lingering pain and health issues. And that pain and those health issues led to a sedentary life. And that sedentary life had left him almost crippled, but this man started to follow DDP and his yoga.

He started to do it every single day. And what he found was ability. He started changing his own life. Even though he had recordings of himself stumbling and falling, he kept trying. At the start of his transformation the man needed crutches to walk. By the end, he was running. The video took off because it was such a raw display of vulnerability and the willingness to put in the effort to change.

That is the feeling you will have as you work your way through this coming process, you will feel crippled. You will feel like things are not the way they are meant to be. That burning sensation within you can either be extinguished with depression and more physical abuse, or you can allow it to burn brighter and power you through the tough moments to come. You can harness that fire to power you through those times where you're going to fall. Because if you're willing to keep getting up, you will find that ultimate sense of victory.

CHAPTER FOURTEEN

Combat Emotional Eating with Stickers??

Don't be like most people. Most people start things and they putter around a bit and eventually they stop because it was too hard. Because they didn't have enough time. Because they got busy. Because their boss was a big meanie. Because, because, because...

Most people have a habit of 'almost' doing things. They almost get there. They almost find the way and they almost get the results. And the life that they've always dreamed of almost within reach. To quote Art Williams again "Almost is a way of life for almost everyone in America. But the winners do it."

My wife Samantha has dealt with her own struggles on her own health journey.

When she was in college, she started eating cookies and chocolate milk every day with her meals. She had every indulgence imaginable and the freshmen 15 became a very real reality for her. It was perplexing because she had always been able to eat whatever she wanted, and she had always stayed lean.

In talking with her family about nutrition on her first college break, they reminded her that most people don't eat three or four cookies and down two glasses of chocolate milk at every meal. For her, sweets had become a replacement for something that she was longing for. This battle continued for the next eight years. When she changed the way she ate and avoided those types of foods, she felt wonderful. But as soon as they were re-introduced, she ran into the struggle. And that struggle was a back and forth battle that drove her crazy. It felt like her normal sweet substitutes, typically fruit, just didn't cut it anymore. She needed the processed food to satisfy the growing craving within her.

She went through this cycle countless times. Certainly, in the hundreds. Here's a discovery that she made after recognizing her pattern and asking the hard questions.

Her breakthrough came with this question:

What makes me feel better?

It wasn't the fact that she had something sugary and delicious. What made her feel better was not having that sweet. She felt awesome because she won that small battle. She had one little check mark on the winning side.

Normally she got a craving, she had the thing, and then felt bad about having the thing. I can remember a family walk where my daughter was running ahead of us and Samantha was talking about how she felt like she had been failing miserably at her nutrition. She had been doing some digging and she came across a friend's Facebook post that spoke deeply to values that they both shared.

She had a breakthrough that her passion for sugar and sweets was her abusing her body. And that the body is a gift from God. And that gift from God was being repeatedly abused by her need for binging food. She was relying on that need for food to sustain her instead of something greater. Many people have moments of breakdown and breakthrough like this. But the most successful take the next step.

They solidify the breakthrough. They make the breakthrough a part of their life.

You already know where your battlegrounds are. You know what's hurting you most. You already recognize where the battles can be won. And those small victories can add so much delight and joy to your life. And that is what my wife started to do. She started recognizing those moments of craving. That was the actual battle. And instead of indulging the craving, she decided to stop. But it didn't work every time. She needed a reminder. She needed something to snap her out of the way that she was used to going about her life. My wife needed a keystone habit that could start to buttress the other habits she was trying to create around eating.

And so, Samantha took action and it was very, very small and subtle. She created a sticker that said, "I am never going to abuse this body that God gave me ever again." That became her rallying cry. She took that sticker and plastered it all over every single tempting food item in the house. She put it on the parmesan cheese that she used to scoop out by the spoonful. She put it on the bag of chips. She put it on the cookies and she even put it on the flour and sugar in the cupboard as a reminder, in case she got tempted to make some cookies.

Her habit is putting those stickers on the new trouble foods that enter the house. It becomes a reminder every time she's reaching for food to check and see if she really wants comfort in another way. That small, subtle reminder hasn't worked every single time, but it has been helpful in winning more battles. To the point where she now actually feels like she's winning the war.

Whatever food is doing for you, whatever need it is fulfilling beyond that basic sustenance, find something else to fill that need, take something else and let it fill that void because no amount of food can heal a broken heart. Find what it is that you're looking for. Oftentimes the foods you crave will point you towards a solution. Let your craving help you determine what it is that you need to be replacing it with and what you need to be working on.

CHAPTER FIFTEEN

Creating Your Own Self Fueling Satisfaction Routine

Something terrible is going to happen to you. You will plateau again. You will experience a drastic slowing down in your weight loss. Hopefully that plateau comes a long time from now, but perhaps it comes very quickly. You may lose a bit and then flat line again. This is not uncommon. And this is why it's important to follow the steps ahead.

Read each one of the habits and projects in the pages ahead. Then choose **one** to work on and work on that one with all your might. Put your energy and focus into mastering that thing. If you try and work on multiple at once, more than likely you'll get overwhelmed, bogged down, and the inevitable ebb and flow of life will tear you away from your ultimate goal.

Pick one and be as stubborn as a bulldog in the pursuit of it.

I've seen my most successful clients follow this type of plan. Remember Tom and Cindy from earlier in the book? They both went through countless ups and downs in the process of getting to and maintaining their weight loss and health. It was their commitment to trying new things and to always be adapting that has gotten them through. ABA: *Always Be Adapting.* That is what got them results. And that is how they keep their results because the same things that got them their results to begin with may not keep the results for the long-term.

Eventually my dream for you is that you plateau again. And that spot where your weight loss stops is actually where you want to be. That plateau is where you have finally lost the weight that you are looking to lose. You have finally reached a place where your body is staying steady at a current weight and you don't regain, and you don't feel the compulsive need to lose anymore.

I hope you find that plateau, but there may be other plateaus in the way before you get there.

I have another client by the name of Michelle. And the first striking thing about Michelle was that she was relatively short. And when I met her, she was quite obese. She has a tremendous smile, a kind heart and a generous spirit. I came to find out later that she had fostered two children and was a biological mother to four more of her own. She is an extraordinarily caring and giving person. She is the type to give of herself before taking care of herself. And her body had paid a high price for it. Michelle had a more difficult struggle than most people.

Her height is an extreme disadvantage to weight loss. Being taller means you get to burn more calories. I am six foot, two inches tall. That means that my metabolism is extraordinarily high compared to Michelle's five foot or less frame. For her to make major change requires a high amount of discipline and an extreme commitment to continual adaptation. And she has had to continually adapt her plan in order to lose the weight that she's wanting to lose. And it's remarkable. Every time I see Michelle, who works out in a different class now, I'm always shocked because she looks different. She looks healthier. She looks like she's in better shape.

During COVID when gyms were shut down and we weren't able to train people in person anymore, we created an online training platform. Michelle took to online training extremely well. When we were eventually able to meet in person again, we did some of the online workouts but in person. There was one routine that was heavily ab focused and I could see most of the class rolling around and stopping for breaks. When I looked at Michelle, she was dutifully pumping out reps like some sort of radioactive super solider.

Some of the most fit people in class would peter out and come to a stop, Michelle continued to adapt. COVID shut the gyms down, but Michelle kept exercising. She found the workout routines not only possible, but she kept doing them. It was a part of her day and she made it a part of her life. She adapted to the change. Many people did not fare so well. So, take a few words of wisdom from Michelle. Keep adapting.

It's almost time for you to jump into the tactics. It's almost time for you to learn the exact secrets for you to reignite your weight loss. Before we get there, we need to pause for just a few more moments.

I want you to feel and experience what is about to happen to you before it even happens. I want you to think about where you're headed. Think about that level of satisfaction that you are going to feel once you accomplish your ultimate goal.

This final point that may keep you motivated in the days ahead. This may surprise you, but happiness doesn't come from things that make you happy.

Happiness, true lasting happiness and joy come from things that you can be proud of. It comes from doing things that bring you satisfaction. Satisfaction is different from happiness. When you are satisfied, you are in need of no more. Often, when we are happy, we may want more of something in order to maintain that happiness.

Look at any alcoholic, shopaholic, or gambling addict, and you can quickly see that humans have a voracious hunger for more.

Satisfaction is the key to breaking out of that cycle. Satisfaction leads to joy. That feeling of unencumbered exuberance that lacks the cynical underpinnings that most of us cling to in order to be 'realistic'.

Satisfaction and joy are where your true motivation come from. You will be satisfied with the work that you are doing. You will be truly joyful because you know the work you are undertaking not only makes a difference today and tomorrow, but you'll be able to stick with it for decades to come. Satisfaction will fuel your future results. When you do hard things, you will feel good about it, and then you'll want to do it again. This allows you to become a self-fueling accomplishment beast. You will tear through things and you will not look back.

In our live classes we give out a survivor t-shirt to people who complete their first month of a bootcamp cycle. Only when someone completes the month, do they get the t-shirt. The smile on that person's face is the biggest I see all month. We give them a t-shirt at the end because at the end it means something. They have accomplished something by surviving to the end of a month. If we just gave them a t-shirt, when they joined, they wouldn't think much of it.

If you get things handed to you, it does not ultimately bring new joy and satisfaction. What we want is that satisfaction as fuel for the results that are coming. When you pick one of the projects or habits ahead to pursue you will be creating a satisfaction machine that will help you create and spread more joy in your life.

CHAPTER SIXTEEN

My Seventh Grade Science Teachers' Sage Advice That You Should Definitely Follow

Up until now, I have been talking about strategy. I have been talking about the broad and general ideas that you need to adopt in order to get to your ultimate goal. From now on, we're going to be talking tactical. We are going to be talking about the smaller things that you're going to be doing that are going to get you to your ultimate goal. The strategy is crucial and essential. You must employ those deep rooted and deep-seated ideas if you want to have any hope of these small changes taking root and having a long-term impact. In Part Two, you'll see all of the ways you can reignite your weight loss. They are divided into Continuous Improvement and Focused Breakthrough categories.

The Continuous Improvement category is where you need to be spending most of your time. It is in this section that you will make the long-term habit changes that will make losing and eventually, maintenance, sustainable.

The Focused Breakthrough projects are designed to create a mental or physical breakthrough. They are short term tactics and can be helpful for getting some quick wins or for getting your head into a better place. Be warned, you may be tempted to spend all of your time on these types of challenges. They are fun and can be done in an hour or a day depending. But short-term wins don't always equate to long term victory.

Before you commit to any one plan of action, I'd recommend looking at them all first. I can remember in seventh grade science class being told by the teacher that instructions were extremely important. He recommended that when we were doing our experiments and when we were doing our homework it was important to read all the instructions before we got started.

After giving us a hearty lecture on how important instructions were, he handed out a sheet of paper to each student, and he said there was a special reward for those that finished first. He told us to get started right away. We threw out the advice that he had just given us and started following the directions one at a time. The first direction said to draw a square. The second direction said to cross out the square. The third direction had us do something even crazier. And by the fifth and sixth direction, our sheets were a mess. I can recall by the time I was on direction five or six out of eighteen, one of the students was already done. I couldn't believe it. So, I read the directions faster. I plowed through and I made it all the way to the end.

When I read the last set of instructions, it said disregard all the previous instructions. When you have read this, put your pencil on the table and sit calmly. When I read that my jaw dropped, I had completely ignored his initial instructions. And I had dived in blindly trying to fumble my way through because I was determined to get there faster. This lesson taught me something very, very important: just because I have the map in front of me, doesn't mean I know how to get there just yet.

I've given you the map. Part One has been teaching you how to read the map and adjust based on the situation at hand. Part Two is the actual map that will get you there. It's up to you to walk the path. Your mission is to read each one of the projects and habits then pick one to do.

I have purposely made them relatively short and digestible. That way you can start to find what your inclinations are and where your biggest opportunities/obstacles are. You may know right away which one is going to work best for right now. But what happens the next time you run into trouble? Eventually your results will plateau again. What will you do then?

By reading all of these habits and projects you will have an idea already of what to do to break through the next obstacle that comes up. And you may even break through that obstacle before it even begins to be an issue because you're applying the other things you've already learned and absorbed. Don't make the same mistake I did. Read all the instructions first before you dive in.

Following a process is remarkably important. It's why we have so much respect for doctors. There's a certain process to becoming one. They don't just hand out medical doctorates. To become a doctor takes a tremendous amount of work ethic, commitment, and knowledge. It takes a commitment to the process.

I can remember a TV show called House M.D. that starred Hugh Laurie as a brilliant rogue doctor who tended to make decisions defying protocol in in an attempt to save the clients life. While much of the time his decisions ended up being helpful, I can tell you, I would not want him as my doctor. His disregard for process and his disregard for hospital procedures would have me extremely nervous about following any of his advice.

Follow the process and you will find the results.

PART II

ACTION PLAN

Did you skip ahead to get here? This is a symptom of what we talked about throughout the book. You're looking for the fast way, for the quick answer, for the immediate results. This plan is none of those things. It is, however, incredibly effective. As I've shared throughout the book, we have clients who have achieved incredible amounts of weight loss success. And it's because of what I talked about during the book.

If you did skip ahead to get here, go back and read Chapter 16, then read the other chapters you may have flipped by. I promise I only made this book as long as it needed to be. There are things back there that you need to hear to find long term success and satisfaction.

Let's set some expectations for reasonable weight loss.

Two pounds per week is pretty fast. That means eight pounds in a month should be the upper limit of what you're aiming for. Once you start hitting above that level sustainability becomes questionable and the possibility of losing muscle should come to the front of your mind.

One pound per week is good. To break that down, a pound of fat on your body is approximately 3,500 stored calories. That means in order to lose one pound a week you must have a calorie burn that beats out calories consumed by 500 calories per day. That's more than a full meals worth of food for most people.

A pound a week is nothing to scoff at. It takes incredible effort to get to that level and you should absolutely be proud and celebrate each pound of change that you experience in the weeks and months ahead.

The process you are entering into is an iterative one. You are going to try something. It may go well. It may turn out poorly. Or you may get some mixed signals. All three of these outcomes are acceptable.

Yes, even getting poor results is useful.

The result right now is feedback. And you are going to use that feedback to make your next attempt even better. Poor or mixed feedback means you'll need to tweak a couple of things in order to get a different result. Good feedback means you may want to double down and do more of what's working.

The Focused Breakthrough section is great for doing one off or short-term opportunities. Each Project is useful, but some may be especially relevant for you.

The Continuous Improvement section focuses on habits and will require you to continually adapt. Plan on committing to one of these habits for at least a few weeks. Adjust the Habit as you get feedback to ensure maximum results.

Focused Breakthrough

PROJECT ONE

Evaluating the Pros and Cons of Being Overweight

Hopefully the title of this one got you to raise an eyebrow. You've probably been inundated with data, ideas, tips, tricks, and reasons why weighing less is vital. It's vital for your health, your mental state, your joints, your heart, etc. But you know what nobody talks about?

Why being overweight is better.

If you are overweight and struggling to lose weight or get healthier it's because being overweight has more benefits to you right now than weighing less.

You may think there are no benefits to being overweight. But you'd be dead wrong.

The goal of this project is to uncover some of the subconscious reasons you may sabotage yourself from getting the healthy results you want so badly.

Take out a piece of paper and write "Being Overweight" at the top.

Now draw a line vertically down the center at the top of the left side write "Pros" and at the top of the left side write "Cons."

Start with the Cons side. You know tons of reasons that it's not good to be overweight. Fill out as many as you can.

After you've done that, head over to the Pros side.

Instead of thinking "Why is it better to be overweight" think "Why wouldn't someone want to be skinny/in shape/fit/toned/muscular?"

What you're going to find, if you dig deep enough, is a list of reasons that keep you from moving and staying on the Cons side of this list. Right now, the pull from the "Pro Overweight" side is winning. And likely it's been winning for a long time. What you're going to need to do is systematically eliminate, prove false, or make inconvenient the "Pros" that you've listed. It's only once the benefits of being lighter far outweigh the benefits of being heavier that you will make consistent progress forward.

For those that are still struggling to fill out the Pros side, here's a quick list of some reasons, I'm sure you can find more.

- When you're heavier, you can eat more food and still maintain your weight
- If you're fit, you're in the minority group, as most people are overweight or obese, that means you'll stand out
- Less body fat means you get cold easier
- There may be extra sexualized attention if you are in better shape, whether from a spouse or from strangers
- You'd need to buy new clothes if you lost weight, and you really like some of the outfits you have now
- You don't want to look "snotty" or "uppity" by being in shape

- It's significantly easier to not work out, try new recipes, or eat healthier
- You really like the taste of junk food and treats

Take the ones from this list that resonate and start to pull apart why that belief has stuck with you. I'd recommend talking it through with friends, confidants, or a counselor. Some of these issues may be much deeper than others and as such may require more advanced help.

The list is just to get you started, but hopefully it reveals your major reasons for NOT getting into better shape. Now that you've created awareness you can begin working at fighting against those beliefs and biases.

PROJECT TWO

Visualize Your Beautiful Future

Remember when we talked earlier about how to get your spouse on board with your weight loss? You need to start off with where you're headed. Talk about the destination and feel and experience how awesome that will be. Have something you're absolutely thrilled about. That is the only way you'll be able to turn down temptation in those tough moments. You'll be picturing your beautiful future while that temptation is in front of you, and you'll know which option is better.

This would be a good one to head to solitary place where you won't be interrupted, light some candles and settle in for thirty to sixty minutes.

Get some art supplies, paper, pens, markers, crayons, paint, magazines, scissors, the whole craft bin if you've got one. It's time to build a vision board. As cheesy as it sounds, this is an incredible method to get clarity on where you're headed and to create a physical reminder of what it is you truly want.

Here's what you're going to do:

The reasons you want to lose weight and get in better shape go beyond just feeling better and being healthier. You want something more out of life. There's a piece missing, and you believe that by losing weight that piece will be found.

I want you to imagine what your ideal life looks like. This is not some I get paid to sit on my butt pipe dream. This is a dream that has roots in what you deeply want. Do you want to retire to a cabin in the woods? Are you hoping to take your grandkids sledding on your eightieth birthday? Do you want to change careers and pursue the thing that makes your heart sing?

Feel free to let your thoughts roll and just start writing or drawing or snipping. Think deeply about what YOU actually want, not what you've been told that you should want. A lake house with a giant boat sounds great, but is it something you truly desire?

Try to create a vision for each of the major pieces of your life. Incorporate your body, your mind, your relations–familial, spousal, and others, connect with your spiritual desires and your dreams of doing good in the world. Bring these pieces to bear on one page. I love using giant easel paper and markers, so I have lots of room to work. But maybe you use a sheet of paper or a canvas. Perhaps you're writing out where you're headed and the feelings that generates within you.

By the time you're done with this exercise you'll have a much better idea of what it is you want out of life. You'll be able to clearly see when to say yes, and when to say no, because you'll know whether it is bringing you closer or further away from your ultimate goals.

PROJECT THREE

Wait

Waiting can be the hardest thing for anyone to do. Just look at a child coming up on Christmas. It can be very, very difficult to wait for the surprise ahead. However, if you are doing the right things, if you are taking the proper steps, if you're pursuing healthy behaviors and you know what you're doing is going to work, then wait.

If you know you're not doing the right things or deep down, or what you're doing is not going to get you where you want to go skip the waiting, go ahead and do something else. Too often, what we find is that people will start something good, but they won't stick with it long enough to see long-term results from it. Many people will start something and pursue it for a day or two or three, or maybe even a week or two.

But when they don't see results after a week, they quit. I would recommend you waiting if you've recently started working on something new. Aim for at least two weeks, possibly three to four, to see if your new habit is actually working.

If you haven't started working on anything new, or you know deep down the change you're pursuing is halfhearted or not all that impactful, there's not as much value in waiting. You probably already know that the thing you're doing isn't going to be that effective. If the thing you're doing is tough, uncomfortable, and is a bit challenging to pull off, there's a better than average chance the thing you're doing will make an impact- If you give it enough time.

Your body is resistant to change, so it may take a bit to see the scale shift. If the change you made is relatively minor, you may look at keeping it going and then adding in something else that can be a major boost as well.

Know this: the change you seek will always take longer to show up than you want it to.

PROJECT FOUR

What Is Holding You Back?

We asked some of these questions earlier in the book, but it's worth revisiting. What is holding you back? If you haven't taken the time to answer this question, do so now list out the things that are getting in your way, list out as many as you can.

Here's a quick list to get you started:

1. My spouse doesn't support me
2. Clients keep bringing junk food to work
3. My mother-in-law badgers me into eating more
4. I never get up in time to do my workout
5. I don't like the taste of vegetables
6. My plan always fails after a week

And now you need to find solutions to those things, holding you back. Once you have listed out what is holding you back, you will start to see what you need to do to break past them.

Here are a few matching ideas to the problems above:

1. Have the "beautiful future" talk we discussed in Chapter 8
2. Throw out the gifted food or take it to an out of the way place where it won't be seen

3. Have a plan in place with loving responses ready to dissuade your mother-in-law from piling more food on your plate

4. Set multiple alarms, work on going to bed earlier, or get a workout buddy that will be expecting you to show up

5. Find recipes that combine vegetables with foods you already love and start eating the vegetables in small quantities at first

6. Figure out what causes the cycle of quitting and work to give yourself the encouragement, support, or motivation needed to bridge the gap

For each problem you write down, spend time to come up with a solution. By having a solution in mind you'll already know what to do when things start to go wrong.

PROJECT FIVE

Reassess Your Habits

Your life is made up of habits. In this project I'd recommend you look at the things that you are doing every day and decide if they are worth keeping. Certain things that you do are going to be worthwhile. Certain things are not worthwhile. Most habits have not been thought through, they just to fill a need.

Have you ever been to a city that grew and evolved naturally? Usually, the streets go at odd angles. Curving streets awkwardly intersect with right angles, and buildings take on a bizarre shape to fill the equally odd shaped lot they are placed on. Compare that to a city that was designed and planned ahead of time. While sometimes monotonous, planned cities are much easier to navigate, and can be efficiently traversed even by a newcomer.

That's the difference between a thought-out habit and a habit that was born out of necessity. If you take the time to think through your habits, you may find that there are more efficient ways to go about your life. There may be ways that you can leverage the things you're already doing and turn them into even better opportunities. If you're already eating breakfast, perhaps it'd be a good idea to make it a healthier breakfast.

Take a pad of paper or make a note on your phone of all the unconscious things you do each day. This will be a difficult task as by nature of it being unconscious, you tend not to think about it. Once you've identified a days' worth of habits see if you can pick out one or two of them to optimize and improve. Maybe it's your habit of mindlessly scrolling on your phone in bed that you notice could be fixed. You notice that some mornings you're just too exhausted to get your workout in. What if you kept your phone charger in a separate room and left it there before going to bed?

There are limitless ways to improve, modify, or shift habits that you already have. It is much easier than building new ones and thus is a great spot to start.

PROJECT SIX

Food Journal

If you are not food journaling right now, I would recommend you do it. Food journaling has been shown to substantially increase weight loss versus those who do not. A Kaiser Permanente study that was funded by the National Heart, Lung and Blood Institute has shown that people logging their food lose twice as much as those who do not. Food journaling is like turning on the light in a dark room. It's essential to find ways to improve. If you don't know what is going on, there is no way to know what to do.

If all you do is journal your food, you may see some results. Journaling combined with analysis is going to be a secret weapon for turbocharging your weight loss. When you log a day's worth of food, it does very little for you. You may get a quick insight the moment you log it, but unless you look at it critically and find room for improvement, the exercise of logging is an opportunity missed. Before you log another day, learn from the first day of logging. See what went well. How was your overall protein level? How many total calories were consumed? What meals were out of balance and what meals didn't have enough protein, had too many calories, or seemed out of place compared to the rest?

Learn from the day that you logged before you log another. That way, your next day of logging can be improved based on what you've already done. This is another example of an iterative process where you will see rapid improvement.

We recommend our clients use the nutrition program Vitabot as it tracks micronutrients as well as macronutrients. This allows you to see if you're actually getting all the requirements your body needs. But this process can be followed using any food tracker. The key is searching for improvement each time you log.

PROJECT SEVEN

Plan for Challenges

We discussed this earlier in the book. If you haven't taken the time to do it yet, it may be a good time to do it now. You need to understand what is going to get in your way and how you are going to overcome it.

Take out a sheet of paper and draw a line vertically down the middle. Label the left side "Challenges" and the right side "Solutions."

And then ask yourself these questions, and fill them in on the "Challenges" side:

Why aren't I in better shape right now?

What is holding me back from eating healthier?

Why don't I exercise regularly?

What prevents me from being healthy?

After going through that list and possibly more if you're already rolling, you can then head to the other side of the page and plan out how you will solve these problems. I promise you this is going to pay off handsomely later. Find a solution to each problem you have presented. I promise you there is a way. If you lack the resources to solve a problem, then you must be resourceful.

In the military, in business, and in your life, planning is incredibly important. I tend to be a 'shoot from the hip' kind of guy and would happily spend much of my life bouncing from one thing to the next. I've missed many golden opportunities because I didn't have a plan in place ahead of time. A plan is not a life sentence, but instead an opportunity to build on something. Deviation from the plan usually becomes a necessity at some point, but that plan points the way forward when the world around you gets murky.

Make a plan for your obstacles, or you'll be left groping in the dark when the obstacle inevitably finds you.

PROJECT EIGHT

Do an Elimination Diet

Hopefully that 'diet' word triggered you a little bit! I hope you sounded the alarm bells and were on full guard when you saw it. If that was the case, bravo, you have learned well!

To those of you who have gone diet crazy in the past, this is not one that I would recommend.

An elimination diet is usually relatively boring and uncomfortable. And I don't recommend it for most people. However, some people do experience negative health consequences directly from the food that they eat. Some food will cause inflammation or other issues, depending on the person.

Inflammation can be a major obstacle to weight loss as it may artificially hide the progress you are making, or it may slow down the hard work you're putting in.

I've heard of food sensitivities to all sorts of things from meat, to dairy, to wheat, to nightshade vegetables (tomatoes, potatoes, peppers, eggplant), to nuts and seeds. Many people don't realize that sugar as an ingredient can be extremely inflammatory. When my wife eased back on sweets, she discovered that she didn't sneeze and cough as much at night. Her body becomes inflamed any time she has large doses of sugar and her immune system goes a bit haywire.

Often the only way to learn of a sensitivity is to go without the suspected food for a time, and then drastically reintroduce it after a few weeks or so.

You might need to experiment. If you notice that your joints and achy, if you notice that you get tired after certain meals, if you feel like there's a general fatigue in your life that you just can't shake, this may be a good option to try out. It is not for the faint of heart. And it is one where you do want to be regimented. I would only recommend this if you have a serious suspicion that you have a food allergy or food sensitivity. Another thing that may be a sign is if you consistently have allergy issues, a stuffy nose, sneezing, etc. as this may be a sign that your immune system is reacting to what you are feeding it.

The way an elimination diet works is… Exactly how it sounds. You eliminate certain foods from your eating! So, if you're testing dairy, you make sure that none of the foods that you are consuming have dairy in it. You do that for a period of time, usually between two and four weeks. And then after that elimination, you introduce that food in mass, and you experience it fully and see if your body has a reaction to it. If there's no reaction, it's a good sign that the food is okay for you to keep eating.

PROJECT NINE

Carbohydrate Cycling

This is a another 'diet' style project that I usually don't recommend for most people. But for those looking for an experiment to try, this could be an interesting one. Carbohydrate cycling works like this: You eat lower carbohydrate for a few days in a row. Typically, three to six days in a row. Then on that last day, you introduce a high amount of carbohydrates, typically several hundred calories more than normal. Then the next day you go back to the lower carbohydrate eating.

Your body will downshift its metabolism as you restrict calories and reduce carbohydrate intake. In that down shifted state, you will feel less energized and your body will burn fewer calories per day. Adding in extra carbs one day a week will boost your metabolism back up again and you'll feel more energized again.

If you have been dialing back on calories for a long period of time but aren't seeing results anymore, this may be the perfect strategy for you.

This can be a particularly effective way to get your body responding to the food that you are eating. This is probably the most 'diet-y' thing I'll ever recommend, but the underlying principle could be why you're stuck.

The biggest caution I would recommend is in order to have a high carb day you must have lower carb days that preceded it. This will not work if every day or every other day is a higher carbohydrate day. For those counting carbs, aim for under 150g per day, ideally closer to 100g. This is usually the hardest thing for most people, as carbs are typically the foods most people crave.

PROJECT TEN

Frozen Food Breakthrough

This one is only recommended in the direst of circumstances. This is for those who are convinced that they are eating in a way that should lose weight, but the scale is stuck and not moving. This can help open your eyes to what may be going wrong in your nutrition.

Are frozen meals nutritionally sound and helpful for weight loss? Usually not. But they are one thing: almost exactly right when it comes to calorie content.

The way this works is you will eat three frozen food meals per day, one for breakfast, one for lunch, and one for dinner, each consisting of approximately 400 calories. If the calories are different, make sure you're matching up the meals so that you're nearby what you need to be losing weight. For most people that adhere strictly to this plan, you will lose weight. It will get you into a weight loss calorie level, and it should get you results relatively quickly.

If you are willing to go through the discomfort of eating a couple of frozen meals for a few days in a row, this may be enough to shake you out of the spot you are stuck in, and it may help teach you that you are in fact, typically consuming more than you think you are. This is one of the biggest problems people find themselves in. They think they are eating healthily and at a level that should lead them to weight loss, but in reality, they are eating much more than they think.

If you believe your eating is on point and there is nothing that can be improved, yet you're still not losing weight, this may be one to try for a few days. I'd go one week at most. And get plenty of water, because you'll be getting some extra salt!

I CANNOT STRESS HOW IMPORTANT IT IS TO NOT EAT ANYTHING OUTSIDE OF THE 3 FROZEN MEALS. No bites, no snacks, no treats, no creamer in your coffee, and no calorie containing beverages. That is the only way that this will shake you out of your rut.

PROJECT ELEVEN

Study Your Emotional Eating

There are whole books and professions centered around this topic so I'll give you enough to get started, but I'll back slowly away as this one can have a profound amount of depth that may need the assistance of a trained professional (counselor, psychiatrist, psychologist.)

Have you ever thought deeply about what is causing you to eat?

It seems silly. Most people would answer: "I eat because I'm hungry."

But if you are overweight or obese, that may not be true every time.

The triggers that cause you to eat matter. The timing of it, the emotions behind it and the cause of it are often a mystery to many people. Often, we are blown about by the winds of hunger without ever studying where those winds are coming from and how we could stop them from going so far off course. If you find there are certain times of day or certain foods or certain occasions where bingeing or overeating tends to happen, become a student of it.

I would recommend journaling every meal you eat for a day or two. This isn't the standard calorie tracking journal. You'll be journaling on the circumstances surrounding your eating.

Here are some things to keep track of:

- Time of day–Log the exact time if possible.
- Location–Where are you, if it's in your house, be more specific about where in your house.
- Who–Write down who you are eating with.
- What–What immediately preceded the eating. (Conversation with someone, traveling, finished up a chore, etc.)
- Current Emotional State–How are you feeling right now? What is your mood?
- After You've Eaten–How do you feel about what you've just eaten?

Ideally you could do this activity on a workday and on a day off so that you can get an idea where your biggest opportunities are.

This may start to point to some of the unhealthy or unhelpful reasons you're eating which will give you the chance to create habits or systems to work around and through those behaviors.

Continuous Improvement

HABIT ONE

Education and Action Balance

Abraham Lincoln was once quoted as saying "Give me six hours to cut down a tree and I'll spend the first four sharpening the ax." If you can create a more efficient vehicle to get you where you want to go, then that may be the technique you want to pursue. The ax in itself is useless without a person to swing it (action). But that person may be ineffective because they are swinging a dull ax (learning).

The balance between knowing when to learn and improve capabilities versus knowing when to go out and just do it are nuanced, gaining strength through practice. Some people are tempted to sharpen their ax endlessly, but never take a swing. You can see this in the chronic learners who are always looking for a new solution and an easier way to do things. I am guilty of this at times. I can spend all day learning about the best way to launch a product or create a meal, but unless I actually do that thing, I will never have the benefits of having created it.

On the flip side, people that take too much action without learning have their own set of inefficiencies. I know plenty of people who will grind themselves to dust working towards a goal. They do the things they think are going to work and eventually, those things stop yielding results. Yet they carry on, believing that their sheer will is what will take them to their destination. This is the type of person who has chopped so many trees that their ax has become dull and is no longer effective. Perhaps this person would be better served if they dropped the dull ax and upgraded to a chainsaw.

The balance between learning and action can be tough to navigate. This is going to be a constant process where you will need to decipher what to do when you come to a roadblock. Some roadblocks must be knocked over by sheer force of will. Others may require more cunning and the help of an expert. A good way to know which one to go with: try one, and if you don't get the results you are after, try the other way.

Be the person who seeks to continually improve at the lifelong project of self-care. Be the person who is willing to step out and try things, even if it is uncomfortable.

HABIT TWO

Vitamin Levels

There was a popular phrase being tossed around a few years ago "If It Fits Your Macros!" The concept being that all types of food were made equal and 10 grams of carbs from a donut were equivalent to 10 grams of carbs from spinach. Donuts and spinach are certainly not equal. Otherwise, Popeye would have been downing them in equal measure.

The way the you get your macronutrients matters because there are more than just three nutrients. Protein, fat, and carbohydrates make up the basic compounds that our body uses to create new cells. Within those macronutrients are micronutrients. Micronutrients are smaller and more numerous. The trouble with micronutrients is that most people don't get enough of them.

Often, we get enough macronutrients, calories in the form of fat, protein, and carbohydrates, but don't get the required micronutrients to support a healthy body. In our day and age, it is possible to be grossly overfed (excess calories) and still be malnourished (not enough micronutrients). When your body is malnourished, it will push you to consume more. You will seek more raw calories in order to fill in at least part of the micronutrient deficit.

If you want to curb hunger, reduce cravings, and get to losing weight again you need to up your micronutrient intake.

The best way to boost your micronutrient intake is to eat more vegetables. That is hands down the best way to fuel your body, stay full longer, and reduce overall disease risk.

Vegetables also bring with them phytonutrients, which are even smaller and more numerous than micronutrients. There are 25,000, and counting, phytonutrients. Phytonutrients help eliminate cancer causing compounds, assist in cleaning and basic functioning of the body, and reduce inflammation throughout the body.

Why haven't you heard about these little guys before?

You have, but probably in a different way. Ever hear of superfoods? Or antioxidants? That's what phytonutrients are.

Interested in living longer?

Want to lose weight?

Want to feel satiated longer after meals?

Looking to fuel your body for optimum mental and physical performance?

Get your veggies!

Aim for two pounds per day. If you're not hitting anywhere close to that yet, don't panic. Just try to get more in tomorrow. Aim to have some at each meal and as a snack. You'll quickly see how fast they can add up!

HABIT THREE

Plan Ahead

The clients that I see that get the best results are the ones that have won tomorrow's battles before they even happen. You experience numerous battlegrounds in your health and fitness on a daily basis. Your kitchen, living room, and drive to work may all become battlegrounds where you gain ground or lose it, depending on your willpower.

Depending on willpower is like depending on chance to win a war. A good general has won the war before it was begun. The battles that come after that are foregone conclusions. A poor general jumps into battle in the hopes of turning the tide their way. This leads to losses more often than not.

Have you ever said, "I struggle with late night snacking."?

Perhaps you feel like "I'm so busy that it's tough to fit in a workout."

Phrases like these indicate where we are fighting, and often losing, the battle for our health. Let's imagine, for a moment, that you were the Sun Tzu of weight loss. Sun Tzu was a Chinese general who wrote the book *The Art of War* and is generally regarded as one of the most brilliant military minds the world has seen.

"The supreme art of war is to subdue the enemy without fighting."–*Sun Tzu*

If you were to win in these battlegrounds before there was a struggle, what would that look like?

Tackling late night snacking as an example, the battleground becomes your kitchen and your home. The enemy is inside the walls and you must valiantly fight them back. Would Sun Tzu allow the enemy into his house? I doubt that very much.

He would have chosen a different place to battle and nullify the need for this cosmic struggle you go through every evening.

Sun Tzu would choose the grocery store to fight his war. He would take nothing home that he intended to lose to. If you have certain foods that you continually 'lose' to in battle to (ice cream, cereal, sweets, chips, crackers, chocolate, wine etc.) then you want to leave them at the grocery store.

Only bring home what you intend to eat. Imagine that any snack that is brought home will be carried on your body to the next shopping trip.

Once you have brought your good food home, what will you do then?

If you don't have a plan for it, more than likely you will lose that battle too. Once in a while my wife will come home with an unplanned vegetable. Sometimes broccoli, sometimes spinach. If that food is not planned for it will often go bad because we just didn't eat it.

If you want to win more battles at home, you will need to win at the grocery store. A sure way to win at the grocery store is to know what your meals are for the week. Then you can buy for the meals and leave nothing else to chance. Become disciplined in your shopping and you will find less food magically jumping into your cart and ending up in your belly and eventually on your body.

> "If you know the enemy and know yourself, you need not fear the result of a hundred battles. If you know yourself but not the enemy, for every victory gained you will also suffer a defeat. If you know neither the enemy nor yourself, you will succumb in every battle." –Sun Tzu

Your enemy in weight loss is extra calories. You must know your enemy. Know where those calories sneak in. Know when your enemy will appear and be prepared for it. You must also know yourself. When is your weakest time? When will you be most susceptible to increased calorie intake?

Plan your meals in advance in a calorie tracking app. See if it is a 'losing battle' before even fighting the battle! You can use meal tracking as a simulation of the future, instead of a depressing look back at your recent past. This will help you 'know your enemy' and you will also be learning about yourself!

If you want to be more productive, plan out your time. If you want to eat fewer calories, plan out what you will be eating. If you want to be exercising more, plan out the time, place, and exact details of your workout.

HABIT FOUR

Watch Out for Mindless Eating

Have you ever watched a leopard hunt? When they catch their prey, they drag it back to a tree and bring it up to a high place so they can eat in peace. You probably do the same thing.

The living room is the modern equivalent. You go hunting in the dangerous land known as 'the kitchen'. You valiantly open cupboards and search the refrigerator for your ever-elusive prey. Once captured, sometimes after several attempts in the same set of cupboards, you bring your prize back to a safe place in the living room to consume your meal undisturbed. You don't realize you've overeaten until you reach the bottom of the bag, jar, bowl, box, or tub. By then, it's already too late.

If this sounds like your life you are not alone. Even stopping by and grabbing a quick munch of something will add up drastically over the course of the day.

I had a client once who came looking to lose weight. By the end of his third week, he had gained almost eight pounds. Perplexed, we began exploring his eating habits more deeply. He mentioned snacking on trail mix occasionally throughout the day.

He came back the next day with a realization. He was eating an entire bag of trail mix every day. Just by grabbing a handful each time he passed by it. That amounted to thousands of extra calories each day. It was no wonder he added so much weight in such a short timeframe.

While this is an extreme example, it shows how every little pinch, bit, taste, handful, and bite adds up. Even if you're not consciously keeping score, your body is. And if you're stuck, this may be a leading cause.

My challenge for you is to track every single morsel of food you eat for 48 hours. I want you to pick the 48-hour window that you'd least want to track. Y'know, the time where you're paying the least attention to food and spending the most time relaxing. The point of this activity is to create awareness. I want you to start thinking twice before you reach for something.

It doesn't even matter if you're logging in an app or on a sheet of paper. This simple act of logging will be enough to help shine a light on your biggest challenges.

Some tips for defeating mindless eating:

- Don't leave unhealthy food visible in common places (counter, clear cupboards, front and center shelf of the fridge etc.)
- Portion out the amount you want to consume before you start eating. Put what you are going to eat in a dish, and then put the source of the food away.
- For foods that are a weakness, measure them any time you are going to eat them that way you know how many calories you'll be getting from them.

- Don't eat while reading or looking at a screen. I know, this one is super hard. But you will benefit immensely from it.

Based on your discoveries while tracking your food, you'll probably find some habits that need to be shifted. Aim to create a level of consciousness with your eating that allows you to be in control instead of always wondering how things went wrong.

HABIT FIVE

Eat Higher Fiber Foods

Ahhhh fiber. I can only think of one thing when I hear the word fiber, and it sure ain't roses. Dietary fiber serves a number of purposes within the body. We're going to talk about intestines, bacteria, and poop a little bit, okay? Buckle up.

Fiber is a type of carbohydrate that the body cannot digest. Ever see a power bar or other food attempt to sway you with marketing that says because it has fiber it actually takes calories away? This is what they are referring to. There are a lot of ways to classify fiber, so we'll stick with two easy to remember categories.

Soluble Fiber

This type of fiber combines with water. When it does so it forms a gel like substance as it goes through your intestines. This can help to slow down digestion, keeping you full longer. By slowing down digestion it can also level out the absorption of carbohydrates and sugars so that you don't get insulin spikes. When your insulin level spikes it leads to fatigue and then more hunger.

Soluble fiber also has the added benefit of binding with cholesterol in your digestive tract and carrying it out of the body so that it isn't absorbed.

For those that struggle with constipation this type of fiber helps to smooth things out and adds moisture to your stool.

Found in: bran barley, nuts, seeds, oats, beans, lentils

Insoluble Fiber

This type of fiber does not bind with water and adds bulk to your stool. Because it is not broken down very well within the body it can act as a cleaning agent within the digestive tract. Think like a cleaning lady with a broom going through your intestines and hitting all the nooks and crannies. Ahh, fresh!

Insoluble fiber also helps to speed up the collection of waste products in your digestive tract, helping them along so they don't stay too long and cause other problems.

Found in: vegetables, wheat bran, and whole grains

Fiber is wonderful. You're already aiming to get more because it comes in many healthy foods, particularly vegetables. Most people are lacking in fiber, so if you can get more, you'll set your body up to be cleaner, stay satiated, and move the byproducts along in a smooth fashion. The path is simple: get more beans and vegetables (most people don't struggle to get the grains/oats-based fiber).

HABIT SIX

Eat by the Clock

To eat by the clock will require you to have at least a rough plan of what you are going to eat for the day. Eating every three to four hours is a good timeframe to aim for. Often eating at intervals of less than three hours leads to significant increases in calories consumed. Likewise, for gaps larger than four hours. This is due to your hunger increasing dramatically at a certain point after not eating for a while.

This timing will keep your blood sugar at a steady level. Especially if you are consuming some fat, slower digesting carbs and protein together at each meal/mini meal/snack. When you eat by the clock, what you are doing for your body is allowing the insulin and ghrelin levels, as well as other hormones, to remain at a steady pace. When these particular hormones have a spike or a drastic reduction, they cause hunger. And a lot of times our biggest enemy in weight loss is uncontrollable hunger.

Have you ever felt 'hangry' before? Where you are so hungry that it begins to impact your mood? Perhaps you feel like certain times of day are your 'uncontrolled eating' times, where you tend to eat way more than you initially intended to. States like this can happen even when we are doing well in other areas. It is common for people to become hyper focused at work or on a project and enter a state of flow. In this state common signals from the body are ignored until they reach a fever pitch and finally break into our conscious mind.

Take out a piece of paper and write your typical wake up time and your typical bedtime on it at opposite ends. Now at regular three to four-hour intervals write another time slot where you will plan of eating food. Try to have eating something within an hour or so of waking and within two hours of going to bed. Based on your schedule how many times per day should you be eating?

Take the number of calories you want to consume per day and break that up evenly at each of those times. If you ended up with six meal/snack times and you want to consume 1600 calories per day, break that 1600 into six parts. That would mean you'd aim for around 266 calories at each meal throughout the day.

By getting in some protein and some fat you'll ensure that those meals and mini meals will stick with you until the next time you eat.

Slow Down Your Chewing

This one is extremely difficult, so be warned! I am the slowest eater. Every time I go over to my wife's family's house, even if I'm the first one to sit down with a plate of food, I will be the last one done.

I chew rather slowly, and I chew thoroughly and in doing so, I do two things for my body. Number one, I open up the ability for my body to process and digest things better. Meaning I may actually get better vitamin and mineral absorption. Number two I open the door for possibly eating less.

As you eat, your stomach begins to fill. And in that feeling process, your stomach gets to a point where it lets you know how full you are. The amount of time it takes for that signal to get to our brain can take many minutes, sometimes as much as 10 or 15 minutes.

If it's taking you 10 minutes to realize that you are full, how much food have you eaten in the minutes between your stomach knowing you are full, and your brain knowing you are full?

If you're a power eater, you may notice that you can down entire meals before you even feel a sense of fullness or satisfaction. If you can chew slower, you'll get the signal to your brain that you don't need to eat any more with fewer calories consumed. This in itself does not guarantee that you will eat less calories, but it puts you in charge.

The work of becoming a slow chewer is a lifelong one and you may find that some habits are deeply ingrained. I know when my wife is anxious or feeling deep emotions, she eats her food more rapidly. Emotions can impact speed of consumption just as much as how mindlessly you are going about it.

I have a challenge for you. I want you to eat a consciousness meal. This consciousness meal must take THIRTY minutes to complete. No TV, phone, book, or computer—just you and your food. Your goal is to eat slowly and savor each and every bite.

Chew or hold each bite in your mouth for thirty conscious seconds before swallowing. Wait an additional thirty conscious seconds before putting the next bite in your mouth. Try not to eat large mouthfuls at a time. Each bite should be just enough to cover your palette with no bulging of the cheeks.

Between bites, you may sip water or unsweetened tea. For this meal, avoid any sweetened or calorie-containing beverages. Many studies have confirmed that liquid calories do not cause individuals to eat less when consumed with meals. Subsequently, drinking any beverage that contains calories is a bad idea for anyone seeking to lose weight.

You do not need to eat the whole meal. Eat only until you are satisfied or until the thirty minutes have expired, or whichever comes first.

What you may find is that it does not take the whole thirty minutes to be done with your meal and there may be substantially more left on your plate than you are used to.

By doing this you will probably eat until you are satiated instead of full. This is a much better feeling to aim for as being full typically means that too much has been consumed.

HABIT EIGHT

Increase Your Calorie Burn

To accomplish this, you will have to **move more**. If you have a lot of seated habits in your life, these will need to be either eliminated or shifted. Finding a way to be active as a full-time resident of a snowy wintery wonderland for six to eight months out of the year is a particular challenge for me. If my work time is spent seated at a computer and my home time is spent seated at a computer or in front of a TV, I am setting myself up for major trouble.

Did you know that you burn about a half a calorie per minute while you are seated? This jumps to over a calorie per minute just by standing up. That means you will burn twice as many calories standing as you do while you are seated. Daily activity matters.

I used to work for Pepsi and there were two types of delivery drivers. One type of driver was in charge of a side loader truck and they wheeled individual orders into small and medium sized businesses. It is a physically demanding job and lots of movement is required. The second type of driver delivered bulk loads to major grocery stores. This type of driver used a mechanical pallet jack to move the product off of the truck.

What typically happened when a driver switched from a side loader to one that used the pallet jack was a massive spike in weight. Many side loader drivers wanted the ease and comfort that came with the bulk delivery routes but passed up on those opportunities because they wanted to protect their health and weight.

Fitbits, Apple watches, and other wearable technology are helping to push people to more activity. If you have one of those devices and it keeps sending you nagging reminders, don't just ignore it. Make it a part of your life. If you need 150 more steps for the hour, go get them!

Try and find activities that you enjoy that are incompatible with sitting. Make a habit of hiking, consistently tidying the house, or having a standing desk available.

Over the course of the month, these types of changes will not make an enormous impact. But over the course of your life, it could add multiple years. This is the type of subtle habit that makes a bigger difference the longer that it is going on. Don't be discouraged if a new movement habit isn't breaking you out of your current rut.

What will surprise you is how thankful you'll be in ten years that you added a new movement habit to your life. It will make that much of a difference.

Get Enough Rest

Sleep is crucial for healthy functioning. When I am chronically sleep deprived, I often don't realize the effects it has on my productivity, mood, and eating. It's only after I've consistently gotten better sleep that I can see clearly how rough around the edges I was.

So, before you write this one off and say "I function just fine as things are," you may want to try some of the ideas in this section to see if you don't accidentally realize how your poor sleep habits were impacting you.

Here are a few things that happen when you don't get the sleep you need:

- Alertness, attention span, ability to concentrate, reasoning, and problem solving are all reduced.
- Memory will be impacted as your sleep time is also your filing time for your brain. You'll forget more.
- Increase your risk of vehicle accidents, heart disease, heart attack, heat failure, irregular heartbeat, high blood pressure, stroke, and diabetes.
- Reduced sex drive.
- Can be a contributing factor in depression.
- Your skin will age faster.

- Hormone shifts that lead to increased hunger and weight gain.
- You'll lose touch with how impaired your functions are from lack of sleep.
- More hours awake means more hours for eating.
- Your metabolism will downshift, and you'll burn fewer calories and have less energy.

Sheesh. You need between seven and nine hours of sleep per day. If you are getting six or less on a regular basis there is a good chance that you don't even notice your impaired function, and thus don't feel the need to make any changes.

Ready for some sleep? Here's some tips to make your sleep time more beneficial:

- Set an alarm to get ready for bed.
- Leave your phone charging in a different room at bedtime.
- Don't look at screens within an hour of going to bed as they can make you feel less tired.
- Take the TV out of your bedroom.
- Use blackout curtains, as your sleep time falls during some hours where there is daylight.
- Keep paper and pen next to your bed and write down the things that keep your mind racing.
- Listen to white noise at night.
- If you are unable to sleep due to anxiety you might be better off getting up, working through the anxiety in another room using different de-stressing techniques, and then return to bed and try to sleep again.
- Make your bedroom a place for sleep. You want your body and brain to associate very closely to particular things when you're in the bedroom.
- Create a bedtime routine and stick to it.

- Instead of sleeping in later to catch up on sleep, go to bed earlier.
- Try and go to bed nearby the same time every night and wake up near the same time each morning, even of weekends. Some people get jet lag every week because their weekends and weekdays are so different.

Give some of these tips a try. You may not even realize how big of a difference it will make until you try it.

Decrease Stress

Your body is wonderfully adapted to handle stress. However, there are different types of stress and they can cause different effects on the body. Over a short period of time, stress can heighten the senses and increase focus and alertness. This is often referred to as eustress, or positive stress.

Positive stress can come from deadlines, obligations, and commitments. This stress takes can take you to a whole new level of productivity and effectiveness. In school I'd often wait until the last minute to work on assignments so that I could capitalize on this type of stress. The problem with this method is that if things go wrong, it could quickly lead to distress.

Distress happens when we feel there is no way out or solution to the problem at hand. When there is a solution, we can be motivated to tackle it. When things seem hopeless 'bad' stress is the result.

In the short term, both good and bad stress and not that big of a deal. They come and go like most other things in life.

What causes a problem is long term stress. And this is often what is referred to when people say they are stressed.

The list of problems caused by long term stress is long, but the one that we're focusing on is this: weight gain. Your body will be primed for weight gain and your mind will be primed to look for relief. This is the perfect marriage to mess up your weight loss plans.

The process of working through long term stress is complex and nuanced. Each person's situation will require a different tactic. I'll explain a few of the most common causes of long-term stress and how you can go about relieving it.

Incongruency

When I graduated college, I had only one job offer. It was the tail end of the recession in 2010/2011 and jobs for young people like me were scarce. I took a sales job at Pepsi, even though I wasn't particularly thrilled by it. As a non-soda drinker and budding exercise enthusiast I thought the stuff was poison.

For almost two years I struggled in that job because my beliefs were not lining up with my actions. It was incongruent. It didn't match. I felt stress just going to work because I felt like I was a part of the process in creating obesity and was the root all the problems that came with that. I found ways to cope, none of them particularly healthy. By the time I was released from that job, I was in the worst shape of my life.

The solution to my problem was simple: find another job where my morals and ideas lined up with the company! But in my mind, there was nothing else out there and I felt trapped.

If you are in a similar situation it can be easy to start to believe there is no way out.

I have obviously changed careers since Pepsi, and I'm here to tell you, living a life that matches up with your beliefs is wayyy better!

Think of me as you from the future. I'm here to tell you that the change won't be as bad as you believe it to be. The pay cut won't be as big as you'd imagine, and the stress reduction has made you the best version of yourself to date.

Take the plunge and find those areas of your life where you're living incongruently and make the hard changes. They'll turn out to be the best thing that's ever happened to you, I promise.

I could just make a list here of some common stress reduction techniques, but you know what? Most of those are temporary. You need to tackle the real things that bring stress into your life. Below you'll see an incomplete list, but there's enough here to get you started on truly ridding yourself of these long-term stressors.

Relationships

People problems are at the root of many daily dilemmas and stresses that we face. It is our relationships that can bring us a tremendous amount of joy, and it is those same relationships that can bring you lower than you thought possible.

I find in many of my clients that they fear one thing above all else: loss of love. That imagined loss of love causes people to do all kinds of wild things to protect themselves and guard their course of love.

One common behavior is for people to project a particular image to the world. They create and cultivate this image of themselves that they believe others will like and then parade around as that masked self when they interact with people.

The way you receive compliments is a good sign as to how dependent you are on your mask. When someone says something nice about you, what is your first response? Most people feign humbleness and shoot down the compliment as if it was an enemy fighter pilot come to destroy them. This is so common it is often overlooked but it points to the mask.

What happened was, someone noticed your mask and said something nice about it. You, knowing that the thing being complimented was there to make you appear a certain way and is not necessarily a true reflection of you, reject the compliment because you know it is actually not a reflection of who you really are.

Do all people who dye their hair, wear nice clothes, and look 'put together' have a mask on? Certainly not.

What matters is living authentically. If you dye your hair, why do you do it? Do you do it to fit in? So that you don't look old? Or do you do it because you like that color better and it brings you joy? If it's the latter, own that.

Being authentic means showing some vulnerability. And the level of vulnerability you have should be a reflection of the people you're with. Among strangers it can be quite odd to see a person's vulnerabilities right away. Vulnerability must be earned. In the same token, to not become more vulnerable around people who have earned that trust comes as a rejection.

I can remember a friend of mine from college opened up to me and told me his life story. It was full of ups and downs and plenty of things he wasn't proud of. At that time in my life, I was incredible shallow and not at all self-aware. After he shared, he looked at me expectantly.

I didn't know what to do. I was so stuck to my persona that I had created that I didn't recognize a difference between the persona and myself. I had no idea I had problems and had not taken the time to flesh out my own journey. My response was lackluster, and it damaged the relationship.

Being authentic and vulnerable around those who have earned that place is like a physical push. You are creating distance with people, and you may not even know it.

If this is an area you struggle, I'd definitely recommend Brene Browns books as she has done a masterful job of fleshing out this topic.

Financial

This category is actually closely related to the two we've already talked about, but I'll give it its own space just because that's how you may recognize it.

We live in a consumer-based society. Our economy thrives on its citizens using their disposable income to buy the next latest and greatest things. Often these things are purchased with money that people do not have.

People borrow against their future earnings in order to enjoy things now. What that means is, future earnings had better not change, or you'll be in trouble.

Unfortunately, things do change. And those changes are not always expected, and certainly not always welcome. I did not see a reason why my income would ever drop drastically from where it normally is. But when the pandemic of 2020 hit, it certainly did.

My wife and I have taken many precautions to make sure we can live off of far less than we earn. Many people, and you may find yourself here today, are one job loss away from financial ruin.

That means your ability to put food on the table, to have a roof over your head, and to provide the basic needs of your household is at the whim of your employer or of the market. Talk about stress!

If you are unfamiliar with Dave Ramsay's work, I'd strongly recommend you take a look. He goes over the baby steps to financial freedom and his capstone course is called Financial Peace. Talk about a dream. If you're living in a financial nightmare where you're subject to the whims of others, you have the power to change that.

The changes won't be easy, but it will be well worth it, especially when your stress starts to go down.

Inputs

The last topic we'll cover is what you're feeding yourself. Not in the nutritional sense, but in the mental sense. The things you allow into your mind will affect the way you think, feel, behave, and interact with others.

When disaster strikes, what do most people do? Once they are in a safe place, we begin to obsess about that safety. After 9/11 my whole family and everyone I knew was glued to the TV for weeks. The same thing happened during the COVID-19 pandemic. People begin to develop new media consumption habits when things like this happen.

Ever hear the slogan "If it bleeds, it leads."? This means that if you're a news company looking for more eyeballs, you'll get those eyes by putting the most horrific and scary stories out front. In the era of social media, viral videos, and news conglomerates, news has been reduced to a simple phrase: pay per click.

If a 'news' company can get eyeballs on its page sit will generate revenue. Fear based media and misinformation have exploded in the past ten years. This has a very real psychological effect on those that consume this media. Living in a constant state of fear or general worry has negative health consequences like we talked about earlier. It also drives cynicism, distrust, and drives wedges between people.

Guard your inputs. That is your eyes and your ears. Be conscious and careful with what you are allowing to shape your head space. If you're convinced that you are in the right and feel deeply convicted about an issue, consider this: there is someone smarter, better educated, and more knowledgeable on the subject than you that believes the complete opposite. Does that mean they are crazy or off the rails? That's what your inputs would have you believe.

But the truth is somewhere much closer to the middle than you are comfortable admitting. And that boiling crisis that seems ready to tear the world apart, might not be remembered in a few years.

I typically don't recommend diets or fasting. But a media diet or fast may be what you need if you find your mind has been captured by the things you're consuming. As I'm writing this book, I'm in the midst of a 90-day news, social media, TV, and video game fast. My stress the last few months leading up to now has been some of the most intense I have ever experienced. I don't have control of other people's actions, of the economy, or of a virus, but I do have control over what I allow into my own head. And I am choosing to own that space, not rent it out to someone else.

HABIT ELEVEN

Drink More Water

What if I told you that your sugar cravings were caused by dehydration instead of a lack of willpower?

Let's get into the science of it, in layman's terms.

When we consume carbohydrates, they are broken down within the body. Some of it goes into medium term storage. This is called glycogen. Short term storage is in the blood and we call it blood sugar. This impacts hormones such as insulin. Long term storage is body fat. All three of these places are important and needed in the proper quantities.

Long term storage takes a while to access. Our body has a relatively consistent level of fat burning that goes on all the time. Often, we don't notice it because it is easy to gain more fat in a day than this system burns. Long term storage is like a pension check. It arrives at the same time and place and in the same amount. If you need more money, you'll need to look elsewhere.

Short term storage, blood sugar, is like cash in your pocket. You can use it right away. But you'll be running some risks if you keep too much on you at once.

Medium term storage is like a bank. You can keep your money there safely and get it when you need it. In this scenario, instead of swiping your card to get money, you need to give some water to get the stored energy, in the form of glycogen.

If you don't have water to trade, your body will try and get some quick cash by making you crave carbohydrates that will put a sugary infusion into your blood to solve the problem of needing sugar to run things, but not having enough water to access your sugar bank.

Your hunger pangs and carb cravings can often originate from a simple source: lack of water.

Lack of water can also cause: bad breath (diminished saliva production means more bad bacterial growth), lead to darker more odorous urine and an increased risk of UTI's, fatigue as your blood sugar drops, the body functioning less efficiently, lowered immune function, skin issues such as dry skin, an increase in wrinkles, constipation, and other digestive issues.

Water is crucial for you to be at your best. The exact amount is hotly debated and is closely related to the types of foods you eat. If you're consuming more foods high in water content, you may not need as much water. For our clients we generally recommend half your body weight in ounces of water. Meaning if you weigh 150 pounds, you'd be aiming for 75 ounces of water each day. That's about four and a half water bottles or about nine 8-ounce glasses of water.

The next time you have a craving, aim to get some more water in first and distract yourself with something. You may find the craving completely disappears.

Here are a few tips that many of my clients use for getting more water in each day:

- Have a glass of water with each meal
- Bring a water bottle with you everywhere
- Drink 16-20oz first thing in the morning
- Get a giant water bottle, 64+oz, and it'll be easy to see how far behind you are for the day
- Schedule certain times during the day as 'water chugging' times (2-3pm is a great time for this)
- Add natural flavors such as cucumber, lime, or fruit to make it tastier
- Use your potty breaks as a water reminder, some goes out, more comes in
- Get a smart water bottle or an app to track it
- Have a glass of water to balance out each cup of coffee or alcoholic beverage

Start Working Out

When most people start a new workout routine, they go from totally stopped to top speed in a matter of days. It is imperative to your long-term health and long-term success of this habit, that you start more slowly and methodically.

We've already talked about the concept of burnout, which is a very real issue with exercise. It's also important to be taking steps against injury. Even a minor injury could put your exercise habit in jeopardy of never getting off the ground. Many people will get hurt in one part of their body, but then not know how to exercise without reinjury, so they don't exercise at all. The lack of exercise makes the person more prone to injury and the cycle begins again the next time they workout.

I'd recommend starting small and adding in ten minutes or so to each day. Pick a time of day and a place you'll be doing it and eliminate as many obstacles as you can to make sure that time and place is sacred. Don't let laundry build up on your exercise equipment, put out your workout clothes the day before you need them, have a dedicated water bottle that you use for your workouts. By doing these small actions you'll set your workout up to flow smoothly and more consistently.

Working out can be a huge boost to your metabolism, both in the short term and in the long term. In the short term, exercise will help you burn more calories and tends to curb your appetite immediately following the workout.

In the long term you'll be able to maintain and possibly build on the muscle you already have. This acts like a free bonus calorie burn just for being alive. It's like living in Alaska, where you basically get paid to live there.

Getting a workout plan together is not exactly easy. Expert advice here can be extremely helpful. You may hire a personal trainer to design a routine for you based on the equipment you have available. If workout planning is not something you want to get involved with, look to join a workout class or an online program that can handle that portion for you. You want to make it as seamless as possible to make exercise a regular part of your life.

HABIT THIRTEEN

Change Up Your Workouts

The way that we exercise can cause our body to make certain adaptations. This is called the S.A.I.D. principle. It means *Specific Adaptations to Imposed Demands*. It means your body will adapt and change based on what you do with it.

If you change up the demands on your body, your body will need to adjust. If you've been doing the same exercise DVD for months on end it's time for a change. It is important to cycle through and attempt different things. If you are a runner, perhaps you try cycling for a season. If you are a cyclist or you're used to high intensity interval training, perhaps this shift to a new form of training.

Changing up your fitness routine can be a highly effective way to improve your overall results. Changing it up too frequently, however, does not give your body the opportunity to fully adapt to the new changes you've made. So, a brand-new workout and workout style every day will not be helpful in getting your body to change for the long term. You need a combination of consistency and change.

As far as a strength training routine goes, the science shows that people get the best results when they are continually attempting improvement throughout a three-month lifting period. So, doing the same strength workout many times is okay, especially if you're making focused attempts to improve. However, after two to three months, you will see a drop-off in return. A change in workout method is needed to continue to see results.

We cover all this stuff for you in our programs, check out the Next Steps section to see how to get involved.

If you're set on doing this on your own, try and plan out your year in four major chunks. With each chunk try to have a new style or type of strength training and each session try and improve on what you did last time. Tracking is especially helpful here. Whether you track weight, reps, of how long it takes to finish the exercise, you'll be able to quantify your fitness and work to improve it.

By changing your workouts at the right intervals and by continually improving at your workouts you'll reignite your progress and start to see change again.

HABIT FOURTEEN

Eat Enough Fat

Contrary to popular belief, fat does not necessarily make you fat. Like most things, quantity and quality play a role. Even if your goal is to shed body fat, you will still need to consume fat daily from your food. There are essential building blocks within your body that need a steady intake of fat. There are also certain vitamins, A, D, and E, that are fat soluble and are only absorbed when fat is present with the vitamins! That means avoiding fat could cause you to be nutrient deficient, leading to many more problems.

Fat is not a bad guy. But fat can get out of hand in a hurry. Carbs and protein have four calories per gram. Fat contains nine calories per gram. Translation: fat is an efficient way to get extra calories. It makes foods 'calorie dense' which means they take up a small area but have a lot of caloric punch. Foods that are calorie dense are more likely to be overeaten because we rely on the volume within our stomach to guide us on when to stop eating.

Fat does play a role in feelings of satiety. Have you ever had a salad with little or no fat? If you're like me, you're rummaging the cupboards for something within thirty minutes because you're just not quite satisfied. Fat adds that layer of satisfaction to our fullness.

Another thing to be wary of is deleting fat from your food in a bid to be healthier. You can see this in foods labeled low fat, no fat, reduced fat, fat free etc. All of these words mean particular things and they tend to give off a healthy aura around the foods they are put on. Don't be fooled. The human body loves a few things: fat, salt, and sugar are the most common and cheapest taste factors that can be satisfied. If you're getting less fat you'll almost certainly be getting in more sugar and more salt in order for the food to still be appetizing.

Sugar is going to drive your hunger as it is quickly digested and causes a spike and crash in your blood sugar. This will inevitably lead to overeating throughout the day. By having food that still contains fat you'll be more satisfied when you're done eating it, it will digest more slowly, and keep you full longer.

Aim to get about 10 grams or so each time you have a meal or snack. That means between forty and sixty grams per day is a good number to shoot for. That means 360-540 calories per day will be fat. Don't worry, just be aware.

HABIT FIFTEEN

Increase Your Protein

There are three macro nutrients: protein, carbohydrates, and fat. We tend to get them in certain proportions to each other. When protein levels are low, that automatically means that you'll be eating more fat and more carbs. If you raise protein levels up, while keeping calories consistent, you'll naturally have to eat less fat and particularly less carbs.

Most carbs that people consume bring with them very little in the way of nutrition and assistance for the body. A few examples of empty carbs are bread, pastas, cereals, chips, muffins, cookies, crackers, bagels, donuts, pancakes, ice cream, pizza, rice, candy, alcoholic beverages, juice, soda, and all the little bonuses you put in your coffee.

Now that I have exhausted the list of all the tastiest things to eat, what's even left!?

These types of foods *are* delicious, and I'm not going to tell you to never eat them. However, from a purely utilitarian standpoint, these foods are standing in the way of your weight loss. They bring empty calories and very few other bonuses with them, despite what their packaging may tell you.

If you took a few of these types of foods each day and replaced them with protein packed foods you'd experience three major things.

The first is a reduction in blood sugar spikes. When you consume these types of simple carbs they are quickly absorbed by the body and go directly into the blood stream. Insulin gets released to tell the new sugars where to go, often going to long term storage (fat).

Because the rush of simple carbs came all at once, your body overreacts to the sugar increase and puts out too much insulin, which causes your blood sugar to drop too low, which causes you to get hungry again sooner!

Obviously, that's not a great strategy for weight loss. So getting off of that blood sugar roller coaster will save you a boatload of extra calories each day.

The second thing that happens is the slowing down of your digestion because of the protein you consumed. Protein takes a lot more work to break down. Everything you eat needs to be broken down so small that it is a liquid.

If you took one of the empty carbs from the list I mentioned earlier and put it in a glass of water, after an hour it would look like a gross fuzzy mass of what it used to be.

But if you took a high protein food like meat, fish, eggs, or beans and immersed that in water, after an hour it would look about the same.

High protein foods will take more work, and thus more time, for your body to digest. This will slow down your digestion and keep you from feeling hungry.

The third major benefit is in your recovery. When you exercise, you're telling your muscles to get better at certain things. You'll often experience soreness and discomfort when you challenge your body beyond what you're used to. Your body will then attempt to repair itself stronger. Protein is your go to ingredient for this.

If you're losing weight and not consuming enough protein, your body will rob Peter to pay Paul – breaking down muscle in unused areas to form or repair muscle in the areas getting more use.

By consuming enough protein, you'll ensure that you maintain, or even build muscle, as you lose weight. That way, the weight you're losing is *fat*, and not the all precious muscle that you work so hard to build.

A simple formula for protein consumption is to aim for .64 to .90 grams per pound of body weight. So if you weighed 150 pounds, you'd be targeting between 96 and 135 grams of protein each day.

Many people who are stuck in their weight loss are getting closer to 60 to 80 grams of protein each day. This is enough to survive and cover your basic needs, but it comes with all the downsides we talked about above.

You can get a double whammy of satiety (less insulin spikes and slower digestion) combined with keeping your precious calorie burning muscle if you can get closer to that higher range of protein.

NEXT STEPS

You've read all the plateau ideas. You're taking action on putting at least one of them into effect. You're going to keep on keeping on because you are adaptable, and you are committed. I'd encourage you dog ear the pages of this book where you were particularly inspired as these stories and concepts can refuel you in times of trouble in the future.

And have no doubt, there will be trouble ahead. You may backslide, you may plateau again, and you may find things harder than you expected. That's all a part of the process and you will be better for it. Through the fires of adversity, you will be hammered into shape. Like the blacksmith creating the finest steel, you will come out of your process stronger, firmer, with a foundation built to last.

Use the Projects as opportunities for short-term breakthroughs and use the Habits as your sustainable gateway to making change that lasts.

Continue to hone, tweak, modify, and adjust what you are doing. When things go poorly, you can choose to get frustrated and quit, or become fascinated and dive deeper into learning about yourself and your body.

As you develop in your weight loss journey, you'll notice it isn't a journey solely bound to a number on a scale. It will encompass your whole self as you grow, change, and discover.

To that end, I would highly recommend you check out a few episodes of my podcast, Your Personal Growth, Personal Brand Podcast to take your self-development to the next level. The show covers a wide range of topics but stays centered on tools and strategies you can use to improve yourself.

Episode #78 with Luke DePron – Facts and myths in the fitness industry

Years ago Luke DePron, a Weight Loss and Transformation Coach, took transformation photos of himself for a Huffington Post article. Since then, supplement companies have stolen and recycled his photos as "proof" of their product.

But there's one itsy bitsy little problem: the photos were fake!

For the article, Luke took a photo of himself looking scruffy, sad, and out of shape. Three hours later after hitting the gym and getting ready for some glam shots, he took his "after" photos.

The point of the article was to show how easy it is to use fake transformations and testimonials to sell products.

To this day he still kindly lets companies know not to use his photos!

Luke and I had a blast nerding out about fitness, weight loss myths, and so much more!

Anna Grabow left home at age 16 to pursue a career in ballet.

She's done battle with an eating disorder, helped deliver a baby as an EMT, and spent a lot of time struggling to find her own purpose.

Through each experience she learned more about herself.

She's now dedicated her life to helping and serving others.

We pulled apart the nuance of finding purpose and how to better enjoy the journey of personal discovery.

We talked about how to get better at being vulnerable, how to set better boundaries and expectations with important people, and how to harness your subconscious to build yourself up.

Overthinking.

It's never been a problem for me, and I'm sure you've never been caught in that trap either.

HAHA. Ok now we can be serious.

In the Information and Social Media era, it's easy to get stuck in our own heads. Trapped in thoughts that keep us away from healthy truth, thoughts that keep us away from calmness and serenity, and even thoughts that keep us away from the sensations in our own bodies.

Through a series of stories and short exercises Laura Gavigan takes us on a journey of internal connection where we can shake off the overthinking and embrace the feelings and sensations in our bodies.

Laura is a mindfulness teacher and we do a fantastic meditation exercise at 34:42

CONCLUSION

You have the tools. You've absorbed the mindset. Now, you need action. None of these 26 Ways will work unless you do. It's time to put on your scientist cap and work boots because you're going to be learning about yourself out in the field!

Here a few suggestions to ensure you get the most out of this book:

Use the Challenges to Solve Problems

The challenges listed in the "Focused Breakthrough" section are designed to get you out of a rut. Choose them intentionally and use them as a learning tool. Even if they go horribly wrong, learn what you need to from it and move on.

A word of caution when it comes to the challenges: don't do them one after another just to get them checked off. These challenges can be deeply insightful and that learning can feel exhilarating. This is the brain's equivalent of a quick hit of sugar. It feels good and gets you just motivated enough to do it again. But, by only focusing on challenges, you'll be cultivating the type of behavior that leads people to hop from one diet/routine to the next one without ever seeing real progress. Your physical transformation will happen in the "Habits" section, your mental breakthroughs will tend to come from the challenges. You'll need both for long lasting success.

Commit to One Habit for MONTHS

The biggest mistake that people make with habits is not failure, but giving up. Failure means you didn't do it, or you didn't do it well. Giving up means walking away from it entirely. Understand that you will forget to do your habit. It's entirely possible that you commit to a habit on Monday and have forgotten to do it by Friday!

That is normal. What is critical to your success is getting back into the habit once you've remembered it. The habit is only a true failure if you quit on it. More than likely, it will take a few iterations and small tweaks to get your habit to a place where it becomes a normal part of your routine. You may need to tweak the reward structure, change the timing, or shrink the difficulty of the habit in order to get it to a sustainable place.

Once your new habit becomes as mindless and automatic as tying your shoes, then you can add in another. Adding too many habits at once tends to leave you overloaded and overwhelmed. And when you get busy, you'll revert to your old way of doing things, quickly leaving your pretty new habits behind in favor of the bad habits you're used to.

Find a Community.

Your people. That's what you want to be surrounded by. Those people who can pour into you and encourage you and give you advice based on their similar journey. Community has never been easier to find. Whether it is at the local gym, in an online forum, or via an evening mastermind call, your people are already meeting and connecting. You just need to insert yourself into the conversation.

To become a part of a new community there is one critical rule: show up, and show out.

Everyone is a first timer at something. Even founding members of a group or class had a first time attending. There's awkwardness, feelings of loneliness and exclusion, and the fear of rejection. But by continually showing up, you can become a normal part of the group.

The second part of the phrase is also critical. Show out. When you're there, be your best and do your best. People are not going to benefit from your partial self. Show up as you and don't make apologies for it. If it's a workout class, go to the front row and make some mistakes. If it's an online community, ask some stupid questions. If you're in a meeting, share deeper than you usually do. The right community will embrace you and welcome you in.

Get Professional Accountability

Books, podcasts, YouTube channels, blogs, articles, Facebook groups, etc. are all great for absorbing information to make yourself better. Sometimes, they aren't enough. Getting a professional to come alongside you, encourage you, guide you, and remove obstacles and roadblocks from your path can help to accelerate the rate of change that you could get on your own. The best performing athletes in the world know this and have multiple coaches from different disciplines guiding their critical routines and training.

You are world class. Perhaps not a world class athlete yet, but you are one of a kind and deserve to be the best version of you that's possible. The hardest part of getting professional help is admitting that you may need help. After that, the rest of it gets easier.

As you're searching for someone or someones to help you on your way, find a professional who isn't desperate to take you on as a client. Look for a trainer, nutritionist, or therapist who is happy to work with you, but doesn't *need* to work with you. Those experts typically have a strong backbone of clientele already, they've learned what works and what doesn't, and they won't compromise on the critical components just to keep you on as a client. Look for honesty and integrity above all else, and you'll find coaches and mentors that can speak into your life so that you are forever changed for the better.

Lastly, remember that this is a journey you're on, not a destination. Weight loss is a great result to have, but eventually you'll get to a spot where more weight loss is either impossible or not worthwhile. Once you get there, your work begins again. Cheers to the journey!

If you found this book helpful or have questions, you can reach out to me at: andrew@andrewbiernat.com. I'd love to hear your story!

Made in the USA
Monee, IL
19 July 2023

39556530R00103